D1403429

Before Disrupting Healthcare

Pallav Sharda

Before Disrupting Healthcare.

www.beforedisrupting.com

Copyright © 2016 by Pallav Sharda

ISBN-13: 978-1532923869

ISBN-10: 1532923864

All Rights Reserved. No part of this book may be reproduced or transmitted in any form or by any means without written permission of the author. For inquiries e-mail contact@beforedisrupting.com.

Table of Contents

1

Preface

1.1. About This Book

Disrupt. One can find that word increasingly associated with healthcare, surfacing frequently in most conference panels, hackathons, product descriptions, and media stories.

Picture a mind-numbing market with high barriers to entry, spiraling costs, long sales cycles, and complex regulations. Then imagine tiny sparks of innovation that are "disrupting" the status quo and transforming everything for the better. What's not to like in that vision?

Regrettably, it's not happening that way. The technocrats have arrived at the gates of healthcare, to be sure. The last decade has seen an unmistakable surge of visionary entrepreneurs hacking 'away at issues related to health. With $4.5B invested in digital health companies in 2015, the venture capital ecosystem also seems equally enthusiastic. But real progress has been slow, almost imperceptible—more like a Darwinian evolution rather than some radical, game-changing disruption.

You may wonder why. It's not because the entrepreneurial wave lacks the required talent or commitment. Many have performed exceptional feats of wizardry elsewhere, overturning the status quo and creating new paradigms. But when it comes to health, big names have floundered. For example, consider the missteps of Google Health (introduced in 2008 and cancelled in 2011), Revolution Health (founded in 2005 by AOL's ex-CEO Steve Case and shut down in 2010), Bosch Healthcare (created in 2008 and closed shop in 2015) and GE Healthcare IT (exited the enterprise Electronic Health Records market in 2015). Countless other smaller startups have failed entirely or captured only an insignificant fraction of the addressable market.

There is an important difference between healthcare and other industries: Its commercial nature is entangled with personal, visceral emotions about life and death. To disrupt healthcare, incoming entrepreneurs must *focus* and *prepare* to a level not demanded in any other industry.

1.1.1. Focus: Choosing Problems Wisely

In entrepreneurship, disruption is glamorous. To be the one who thought outside the box and executed at such massive scale that the whole landscape shifted. But before taking on the health industry, one needs to step back and assess the priority of the target. Is it even worth disrupting?

Industry outsiders most likely lack sufficient insight to gauge the priority of healthcare issues. They tend to focus on a particular technology and hunt for healthcare problems to solve with it. For example, consider the recent emergence of companies seeking to force-fit Google Glass to health applications. But the exploration should be the other way around: Focus on the healthcare issue and search for its technology solution.

Regrettably, in the absence of actual healthcare experience, the fantastic talent and passion of incoming entrepreneurs gravitates to the less important areas of this troubled industry. Having said that, the "healthcare experience" need not be professional training as a doctor or nurse. Even suffering a serious health issue (yourself or someone close) can thrust one deep enough into the care delivery labyrinth to clearly sense its priorities.

The entrepreneurial spirit behind all ideas, irrespective of their importance, is admirable. It takes courage to follow one's heart and withstand criticism from others. Surely most (if not all) health-related startups have motivated and well-intentioned individuals behind them. It's also true that most startups pivot direction multiple times to ultimately reach a viable and worthy cause, so initial focus is not necessarily the final one.

But good intentions can't serve as justification for unfettered and ineffectual attempts at reimagining healthcare. The current mess consumes more than 17% of our GDP, and there is an urgent need to course-correct it. Our shared society bears the time and expense of incubating talented individuals with the ability to change the status quo. We should all be concerned with the opportunity costs of which issues those innovators tackle first.

Unless they have really strong domain expertise and previous experience, most investors indulge only in the areas of the healthcare industry they can understand. This rules out the complex, entrenched areas which desperately need innovation and rethinking. Media tends to publicize anything that sounds exciting, irrespective of its merits. The result is a lot of noise, misconception, and misalignment about health innovation. Underneath it all, we continue to have a stolid health industry that is fundamentally infantile in technology uptake. Most of the corporate new-effort bandwidth goes into conventional areas like billing and reimbursement, because those applications are the easiest to comprehend and monetize.

We need stellar startups that reinvent the truly problematic aspects of healthcare. The "medical-grade" problems that affect the daily lives of the patients who utilize hospitals and clinic services, and the providers who care for them. For example:

- Health records with intuitive user interfaces that digest and beautifully display the impending avalanche of omics data.

Publishing and sharing health records should be as easy as blogging on WordPress or contributing to a Wiki.

- Domain-specific Decision Support Systems that can be added to existing systems, like browser extensions added to a web browser. A marketplace (like iTunes) to distribute such solutions.

- Personal Health Records with true zero-effort adoption and complete patient ownership. These should work well on mobile, share easily, and update automatically.

- Consumer-centric apps that help prepare patients for major clinical interactions like surgery, by providing educational content, virtual tours, and checklists.

- Artificial Intelligence systems that help providers prioritize the incoming data streams (emails, lab results, referrals) in accordance with the urgency and complexity of the case.

Not all is lost. There are a handful of startups that have gone beyond concept arbitrage to tackle worthy issues. Simplee.com is deciphering cryptic medical bills. KitCheck.com is making drug inventory management more modern. HiOscar.com is an innovative, technology-centric health insurance company. Flatiron.com is organizing cancer data and rethinking oncology care. OmadaHealth.com is creating a platform for preventing and managing chronic diseases. OneMedical.com is creating a modern primary care experience.

As J.K. Rowling has written, "It is our choices, that show what we truly are, far more than our abilities." Superior technological abilities don't mean much if one chooses to work on the insignificant, and appreciate the unimportant.

1.1.2. Prepare: Knowing Beforehand

Tech innovators like to describe healthcare as a pitiful cesspool of orthodox people and organizations with their heads stuck in the sand. Strict hierarchies, twisted politics, change resistance, tech ludditism: Pick any mangled aspect of doing business in health and you can easily find supporting evidence and a litany of personal anecdotes from those who have worked in the space.

But the vast majority of individuals working in the healthcare industry didn't intend for it to be this way. There is plenty of healthcare talent and vision that constantly tries to course-correct. Aspiring health entrepreneurs need to learn about what goes on in the trenches of the actual system before embarking on an expedition to reinvent it. Without that preparation, there is a significant risk that the only thing they will change is their own mind about the merits of pursuing healthcare disruption.

The transformative power of technology is celebrated in spaces like social networking (think Facebook), communication (Apple), transportation (Uber), and lodging (Airbnb). But using that power as an excuse to not learn the fundamentals of an industry is a bit foolhardy. Failure to understand the incumbent forces in healthcare is probably the biggest reason startups fail to gain traction. In order to transform healthcare, one must work *with* the system.

This brings me to the reason for writing this book.

My goal was to write a simple guide for the brave individuals who have decided to venture into the frigid waters of healthcare. I truly believe that if the smart people who want to disrupt healthcare learn about the industry's existing state, they can calibrate their vision and execute better.

This book is based on facts, anecdotes and insights gathered during my adventures with health technology. Having had the good fortune to see the space from the perspective of vendors, providers, insurers and startups, I can show readers the landscape from a high vantage point.

Readers who can benefit from this book include anyone:

- Interested in creating (or investing in) a health information technology offering

- Mostly unaware of the inner workings of the industry (that is, an outsider)

- With a previous or current background as an engineer, product person, investor or entrepreneur

If you want to understand the big picture of current healthcare information technology market, this book is for you.

1.1.3. Caveats

In writing this book, I assumed that intelligent individuals only need high-level directional guidance when learning about complex spaces. The necessary details are easier to find when the problem space's foundations are clear. That is why this book takes the macro-view throughout, deliberately avoiding the nitty-gritty and giving only select examples. If you want comprehensive lists and exhaustive details, you'll surely be disappointed.

The opinions and conclusions expressed in this book are solely mine. I dislike cliché consulting-grade answers like "It depends" or "Yes and No." Hence, I've chosen to take a stand on polarizing topics, even if that means risking neutrality or political correctness.

The content is exclusively written from a North American market perspective. Because the healthcare market changes so quickly, any book begins to grow obsolete from the moment it is published. Some of the companies mentioned as examples may not exist by the time you read this, or they may have pivoted directions. If nothing else, this volatility gives me hope for a second edition of this book.

Like all mortals with an opinion and the capacity to click on a keyboard, I'm vulnerable to errors. If you find something that is factually incorrect or constitutes copyright infringement, please reach out to me directly.

1.2. Unavoidable Jargon

It's not humanly possible to turn the dull, complicated morass of healthcare into a thrilling read. I imagine you, the reader, to be a passionate do-it-yourself person who is eager to learn more about healthcare and its relationship with technology. Perhaps your motivation will transcend the inevitable trickle of acronyms and complex details. To assist you along the way, a short list of the peculiar syntax used throughout this book follows.

Let's begin with the basics. Aside from patients, there are three other key constituents in healthcare:

1. **Providers:** Those who give care. Physicians, nurses, and almost any other licensed clinical professional you can think of. Synonym: clinicians.

2. **Payers:** Those who foot the bill for care. Health insurance companies, essentially. Sometimes patients pay for themselves, but that scenario is excluded here. Payers always refers to insurance companies. Synonym: insurers.

3. **Policymakers:** Those who make the rules relevant to care. This theoretically includes our elected representatives, but usually refers to the government agencies like CMS (Center for Medicare and Medicaid Services) which are responsible for health policy and programs.

Other terms that you may encounter regularly in this book:

- **Inpatient**: Refers to hospitals and similar facilities where a formal admission is required and stays last longer than 24 hours.

- **Outpatient**: Refers to clinic-like settings. Compared to Inpatient facilities, they provide shorter visits (less than 24 hours), treat simpler conditions, and generally cost less.

- **Health Organization**: A high-level overarching term that encompasses both inpatient and outpatient facilities. It basically means a place where clinical professionals work to deliver healthcare services. Insurance companies are excluded. Synonyms: Care Delivery Organization (CDO), Health Delivery Organization (HDO).

- **Health System**: A vertically integrated health organization that provides all care services within its own network. For example, Kaiser Permanente, Dignity Health, Intermountain Healthcare, and Banner Health. Synonyms: Integrated Delivery System (IDS), Integrated Delivery Networks (IDN).

- **ACA**: The Affordable Care Act. It was signed into law in March 2010, and is discussed further in section 2.4. Policy. Synonyms: Patient Protection and Affordable Care Act (PPACA), Obamacare.

- **ACO**: Accountable Care Organization, a new format for health organizations promoted by the ACA. Discussed throughout section 2.4. Policy and section 4. Health Information Exchanges.

- **EHR**: See section 3. Electronic Health Records. Synonyms: Electronic Medical Records (EMR), Electronic Patient Records.

- **PHR**: See section 3.6. Personal Health Records.

- **HIE**: See section 4. Health Information Exchanges.

- **HHS**: Department of Health and Human Services. The U.S. government office overseeing all federal regulations and programming for enhancing and protecting the health and well-being of all Americans. Nearly 80,000 employees and over 1.1 trillion dollars in authorized budget for 2016.

- **CMS**: Centers for Medicare and Medicaid Services. The part of HHS that oversees the federal Medicare program and works in partnership with state governments to administer other social healthcare programs like Medicaid. Roughly 4,000 employees and uses more than 90% of the HHS budget.

- **ONC**: Office of the National Coordinator for Health Information Technology. The part of HHS that leads all Health IT efforts, including grants, policies, and standards. Around 200 employees and a $90 million budget for 2016.

- **MU**: Meaningful Use. The financial incentive program started by CMS to promote adoption of certified EHR technology, under direction of the American Recovery and Reinvestment Act ("Stimulus Act") of 2009. Explained more in section 2.4. Policy.

- **CPOE:** See the section 3.4 Computerized Provider Order Entry. Synonyms: Order Entry, Computerized Physician Order Entry.

- **PCP**: Primary Care Provider. Synonyms: Primary Care Physician, Family Physician, General Practitioner.

- **Epic**: One of the major Electronic Health Record vendors. www.Epic.com.

- **Cerner**: Another major Electronic Health Record vendor. www.Cerner.com.

2

The Landscape

2.1. Health and Technology

Health and technology have crossed paths many times, and in many ways. Today, there are several terms used to define the multiple spaces emerging from their overlap. While sometimes nebulous, these terms do have the power to conjure visions and create communities. So it's worth spending a minute on the key ones to weigh their validity.

Health Tech

Those in the venture capital community have long used "Health Tech" as an overarching term for everything at the intersection of technology and healthcare. "Tech," in this case, is generic enough that it goes beyond just software to include medical devices (hardware) as well.

Health IT

"Health IT" qualifies Health Tech with an information-only context. It has grown to be associated with enterprise-focused, traditional companies that deal with hospital and clinic workflows. Blogs like Histalk.com and ChilmarkResearch.com are good places to learn about the Health IT space.

Despite its enterprise skew, Health IT is both sufficiently overarching and not too vague. The moniker can also accommodate the new developments that arise in the health software domain. For all those reasons, it's used throughout this book.

Digital Health

It's the newest term on the block. Thanks to overzealous and ill-informed media publications, there is an unspoken association between Digital Health and sparkling startups. Anything in health that is massively funded or espouses new-age tech paradigms (like SaaS, mobile, sensor, cloud and social) gets shuffled into this category. For example, Theranos.com (lab company), HiOscar.com (health insurer) and Jawbone.com (consumer electronics) are all considered Digital Health companies by prominent industry publications like RockHealth.com. For an emerging term, Digital Health has managed to find obscurity before viability.

Other terms

There are plenty of related terms being shuffled around as well. "Digital Medicine" is the sister term to Digital Health, describing tech-driven changes in the medical profession. A few years ago, the term "Health 2.0" gained mainstream traction as a way to point out next-generation technologies and startups. I consider it as a synonym to Digital Health. Further hypothetical versioning (Health 3.0, 4.0) is never useful, and should be dismissed as it doesn't really put any real bounds to what is included in a given "version" of Health (or not).

The noise from promotion of multiple overlapping terms ends up drowning out the actual useful niches that warrant legitimate names. For example:

- Telemedicine has genuine specializations, e.g. Telestroke, Teledermatology, Telepathology.

- EHRs are differentiating further into sub-categories like Personal Health Records and Community Health Records.

- Biomedical informatics is one of the key underlying sciences in Health IT, with established sub-disciplines like Clinical Informatics, Public Health Informatics, Nursing Informatics, Personal Informatics (which is a much better name than Quantified Self).

'Given the rapidly maturing industry, it is quite possible that some of the uber-niches may end up making more sense than their parent terms. That's because in fast developing fields, specific use cases are often easier to market and understand than the parent phenomenon. The differentiation between factions is useful to parse market rhetoric, but probably not worth debating conclusively.

2.1.1. The Overall Market

We can categorize the health tech landscape into two broad, high-level segments: Enterprise and Consumer.

Enterprise Health Tech

The average healthcare enterprise is a predictable environment for healthcare vendors. One can always expect enterprises to be political hierarchies that resist change and are slow in IT adoption. System vendors are asked to give details and demos through formal, mind-numbingly long RFIs (Requests For Information) and RFPs (Requests for Proposals) processes. Vendor claims are usually beyond actual capabilities because sell-first-then-build is a common mantra. Sales cycles for large IT projects at hospitals usually span at least 6 to 12 months, and typically require board-level approval. Implementation durations vary from 6 (normal for EHR upgrades) to 18 months (e.g. for EHR replacement) and nearly always run over budget.

The two main building blocks in Enterprise Health Tech are Records and Exchanges.

Records, or more formally, Electronic Health Records (EHRs), are internally focused. A care delivery organization uses EHRs to handle the in-house workflows (like documentation, billing, scheduling, and reporting) of their own information island.

Exchanges are better known as Health Information Exchanges (HIEs). HIEs are externally-focused information systems, purpose-built to connect organizations and facilitate information exchange between them. In general media, the term "exchange" may sometimes refer to Health Insurance Exchanges (HIXs) which are a totally separate phenomenon from HIEs. HIXs are marketplaces for buying and selling health insurance, in accordance with Obamacare. For the purpose of this book, "exchanges" always means HIEs.

A good analogy for understanding the roles of EHRs and HIEs comes from the financial industry. The internal workings of a bank (like customer relationship management, sales, staffing, and record-keeping) require a highly customized local enterprise system, like what an EHR does for an health organization. The inter-bank information exchange, however, requires an Automated Clearing House, which is similar to what an HIE does in the healthcare ecosystem.

Lines blur quickly in the constantly-changing real world, though. EHR vendors have not ignored opportunities to expand into HIE-like functionality. Typically, they do so in the context of exchanging information between multiple installations of their own system across customers. For example, Epic's "Care Anywhere" product is basically an HIE that can connect disparate Epic customers. Similarly, HIEs have tried their hand at providing light-weight EHRs as a part of their portfolio.

But EHRs are mostly in the business of providing an *inside-out* view of health information. Their solution primarily helps with the internal workflows of a health delivery organization and only secondarily tackles the functionality of external information exchange. By contrast, HIEs are designed from an *outside-in* perspective, mainly solving for information exchange between participants, not the internal day-to-day operations of a care delivery organization.

Consumer Health Tech

This is the retail side of Health IT, the aspect that most overlaps with the new crop of "Digital Health" companies. Typical examples are the wearable, sensor-based devices that have recently proliferated (like FitBit.com, MisFit.com, and LumoBodyTech.com). It is important to note that this category is not restricted to just hardware offerings. Software startups that help consumers find the right doctor, price-shop for care, understand their health bills, and get health coaching are some non-hardware examples. Overall, this emerging collection of consumer-oriented health information solutions is attracting plenty of venture capital and attention from conference organizers.

An important distinction must be made between consumers in health and other industries (like packaged goods or automobiles). Healthcare consumers have been conditioned to expect third-party reimbursement for the healthcare services they consume. Wellness enthusiasts may be an exception, but the average sick patient will always have a twofold Pavlovian response when it comes to healthcare services:

1. Is it formally prescribed (or endorsed) by my provider?

2. Is it covered under my insurance?

In those questions lies the Achilles' heel of the consumer-focused health tech industry. It was born in the fertile, unrestricted fields of consumer technology but must relocate to the regulated barracks of conventional healthcare. Cool gadgets and services in health may become viral among early adopters, but their spread into the real healthcare system seems to be less infectious.

Richer, more unified

Like the tech industry in general, healthcare is flush with investment money. 2015 represented a five-year high in venture funding for U.S. health-care companies, rising to a record $16.10B, a 34% jump from 2014. Apart from venture capital enthusiasm and federal stimulus, healthcare also enjoys investment from other industries. Big names in tech keep pouring money into new health forays, like Google's Life Sciences, Apple's HealthKit, and Samsung's S Health. Big consulting companies like Accenture, McKinsey & Company, IBM, and Northrop Grumman have dedicated practices in Health IT. Even wireless infrastructure players like AT&T, Verizon, and Sprint have established formal healthcare groups.

Buzzwords in healthcare are constantly renewed through conferences, high-profile speeches, media and regulations. For example: Accountable Care, mHealth, Population Health, Meaningful Use, Health 2.0, Quantified Self, Big Data, Precision Medicine. The lineup of conferences and hackathons keeps growing, each one a mashup of some tech trend with healthcare. The current reigning events are the annual Health Information and Management Systems Society (HIMSS) conference in February for Enterprise Health IT, and the Health 2.0 gathering in September for Consumer Health IT. Both meetings have reached a size, cost and complexity that their primary utility is now networking, not knowledge transfer.

With more than $400B spent on deals, 2014 was celebrated as the year with the highest-ever level of annual M&A in healthcare, until 2015 blew past that record with more than $600B.[1] And these figures don't even account for the "soft" mergers—the tight alliances—that effectively have the same market result as an outright merger. For example, AllspireHealthPartners.org is an alliance, not a merger, of seven health systems in the northeast with nine million people under care. A similar combination of Anthem Blue Cross and seven top health systems in Los Angeles is VivityHealth.com.

The consolidation trend is bound to slow down in time, but its effects will be long-lasting. Moreover, the lines are blurring between providers and insurers, as both factions try to extend into the other's role. Within the next two decades we will be squarely in an era of tight clinical integration. A handful of narrow networks (resembling Kaiser Permanente) will dominate each state, forcing smaller players out of business. A future featuring a less fragmented market may prove good or bad, depending on the startup and its focus. Hopefully the remainder of this book will help you make your own predictions about how the healthcare market will adjust to constantly changing regulations, incentives, and technologies.

2.1.2. Research Resources

If you want to learn more about the Health IT industry or just keep up with the news, try these:

- MobiHealthNews.com, Rock Health (rockhealth.com/news), and Health 2.0 (health2con.com/marketintel) are the mainstay sites for keeping up with new startup entrants into the healthcare ecosystem. The latter two have a tendency to be sensationalistic and cheerleading so take their reporting with a grain of salt. Rock Health's reports (rockhealth.com/research) usually provide a great overview of overall startup activity.

- HISPros.com/HIStory is an excellent, unbiased, and quirky account of Health Information Systems and their evolution by industry veterans. If you want to understand top EHR vendors, be sure to check out the vendor profiles there.

- HIMSS.org is the industry behemoth that organizes the annual mecca of Health IT. They offer both premium (himssanalytics.org) and some basic free reports (apps.himss.org/foundation/industry.asp) online. The annual HIMSS conference exhibitor guide always features a fantastic directory of vendors. You can access this guide online around conference time. HIMSS organizers categorize the market very well and every company that has something to do with enterprise Health IT is on that list.

- Key industry analyst firms are KlasResearch.com, Frost.com, Advisory.com, and my personal favorite ChilmarkResearch.com.

- The most detailed, passionate, and candid information source is Histalk.com. It's an informal blog with a cult-like following within Health IT circles. Highly recommended.

2.2. Electronic Health Records

2.2.1. EHR, EMR, PHR

Like many tech fields, Health IT is filled with jargon and acronyms, and some of those terms get used interchangeably. What could possibly be the difference between an Electronic Health Record (EHR) and an Electronic Medical Record (EMR)? Parsing the distinction is a fun, easy way to start knowing the space.

First off, the term EMR came before the term EHR. The industry first landed on the EMR acronym, but the concept of computerizing records started extending beyond a particular visit or organization, and a new term was deemed justified. EHR has the privilege of including the entire spectrum of health-related information, rather than just "medical" visits. For example, if the patient was self-noting their subjective symptoms or Glucometer readings in a weekly diary online, that information would turn an EMR into an EHR.

This is a good time to introduce the concept of PHR (Personal Health Record). A PHR represents the patient's personal copy of their medical record. Most PHRs in existence today are connected to an institutional EHR and make selective information from the enterprise record available to the patient. More detail is available in section 3.6 Personal Health Records. An easy way to define EHR is to think of it as EMR+PHR.

In 2008, ONC commissioned an organization named NAHIT (National Alliance for Health Information Technology) to define Health IT terms like EHR, EMR, and PHR. This was about as useful as the FDA paying consultants to create textual definitions of flu symptoms, and the project wound up wasting taxpayer money. The work didn't matter much then, and certainly doesn't matter at all now. No wonder NAHIT closed shop in late 2009.

All this definition and clarification actually has no bearing on product execution. The industry has settled on EHR as the preferred term, especially after the federal regulations explicitly adopted EHR as their term of choice.

2.2.2. A Brief History of EHRs

Before the year 2000

The thought of creating medical records using a computer is more than half-a-century old. The EHR's origin can be traced as far back as the 1960s, when large academic medical centers and some government agencies began considering the idea of computerizing medical data. The University of Utah, Harvard University, the Mayo Clinic, the Department of Veteran Affairs, and the Regenstreif Institute were among the famous pioneers of EHR-like systems.

Unsurprisingly, the need to comply with reimbursement requirements is what drove the development of information systems that digitized healthcare data. Most of these enterprise systems (then called "Hospital Information Systems" or HISs) originated in one of two ways. One group started off as patient billing systems, and then functionally extended to capture just enough clinical information to get the bills out of the door. For example: Siemens Medical Systems (now a part of Cerner.com), and HBOC (bought by McKesson.com). The other group sprouted from best-of-breed niche departmental systems that gradually started to cover neighboring workflows, ending up with enterprise suites. Examples include Cerner.com, Meditech.com, and Epic.com.

Many of the early systems stored information as unstructured text, which made it difficult to analyze. The importance of structured records and automated querying was set forth with the introduction of the "Problem-Oriented Medical Record" concept by Lawrence Weed in 1969. The next several years saw the rise of higher-level concepts like controlled vocabularies and decision support. The decade of the 1970s marked the inception and creation period for the "Veterans Health Information Systems and Technology Architecture" (VistA), the EHR of the United States Department of Veterans Affairs (VA) medical system. VistA was destined to become a legend in the EHR world, with its open-source attitude and unparalleled size.

These initial decades were characteristically focused on hospital (or inpatient) record systems. The financial and regulatory need for clinic-based (ambulatory) records was lower in that fee-for-service era. By the 1980s, managed care had gained enough foothold to shift the model to fixed-price service contracts, so the priority for information systems changed with it. Ambulatory information systems that managed health data outside the hospital setting were seen as essential to providing cost-effective care.

The attention to EHRs increased considerably in the last two decades of the century amidst widespread recognition of its potential to improve health care. In 1987, a not-for-profit organization named "Health Level Seven International" (HL7) was created to develop standards for the exchange of health information. Today HL7 is a behemoth with 2,300+ members;

including more than 90% of the information systems vendors serving healthcare. In 1991, the revered Institute of Medicine (iom.nationalacademies.org) released the first landmark public policy report in this space. Titled "The Computer-Based Patient Record (CPR): An Essential Technology for Health Care", IOM's paper argued in favor of using EHR-like technology, albeit using the regrettable acronym of CPR.[2]

During that same period, ambulatory EHRs started to appear in large outpatient clinics and physician offices. Their functionality was comparable but less complex than the inpatient (hospital) systems, given that outpatient facilities generally handle less critical patients, and in lower numbers. Perhaps because of those very distinct business operations, the interoperability between inpatient and outpatient systems suffered in terms of organizational priority. Information was generally confined to one system or the other, with minimal integration.

After the year 2000

Things started getting more intense with the turn of the century. The public dialogue around EHR technology became more passionate and positive, with a sense of urgency for adoption. In November 1999, IOM struck again, this time shaking the ground under medical community's feet with the report "To Err is Human: Building a Safer Health System."[3] The report included the disturbing and now over-quoted statistic that between 44,000 and 98,000 Americans died each year from medical errors. Five years later, in his 2004 State of the Union address, President George W. Bush launched an official initiative to make electronic health records available to most Americans within the next 10 years. That optimistic roadmap put EHR technology firmly into the collective consciousness of the healthcare market, if not the nation. The Bush administration also created the first government office explicitly meant to deal with health information: The Office of the National Coordinator for Health Information Technology, or ONC (HealthIT.gov) within the U.S. Department of Health and Human Services (HHS).

Another milestone came in August 2003 when Kaiser Permanente, one of the biggest names in healthcare, signed a three-year, $1.8 billion deal with a little-known company from Wisconsin called Epic Systems. That momentous contract was the beginning of Epic's growth from an under-1,000 employee, $100 million annual revenue company to an over-5,000 employee, $1 billion annual revenue giant that claims to hold more than half of America's medical records today. There were initial concerns that the Kaiser contract would break Epic's back, but instead it kicked off a trend of mega-deals in Health IT.

In February 2009, President Obama signed the "American Recovery and Reinvestment Act" (ARRA) into law, providing $787 billion to accelerate the nation's recovery from economic crisis. Tucked in that torrent of monetary stimulus was the "Health Information Technology for Economic and Clinical Health" (HITECH) Act, which allocated $30 billion to assist providers and their entities in adopting health information technology like EHRs.[4] HITECH was an adrenaline shot that raced through the system, and eventually transferred most of the money to vendors. As a direct result, the sheer number of EHR vendors in the market exploded. The number of hospitals with basic EHRs went from 12% in 2009 to 75.5% for 2014.[5] That's more than a six-fold increase in just five years!

This historical perspective shows that EHRs were born to primarily serve financial value propositions for care organizations (like better billing, accounting, and scheduling). The need for a clinical value proposition was secondary in most cases. This creational DNA has continued to influence evolutionary vectors of the EHR industry. The functional maturity and usability of clinical modules have lagged behind the non-clinical ones. Only in the past 10-15 years have both clinical and financial benefits of EHRs begun to share the marketing limelight.

2.2.3. EHR Market Characteristics

The inpatient EHR industry behaves like an oligopoly. That means it's dominated by a handful of big and powerful sellers. The top three vendors (Meditech.com, Epic.com, Cerner.com) account for more than half of the market share.[6] If you include the top 10 inpatient EHR vendors, that share goes to 90%. Knowing the characteristics of such an environment can help predict how it will react to changes.

There are three main properties of an oligopolistic environment:

1. *Interdependence*: The action of one firm always affects the action of another. For example, a PR blitz by one firm around population management will induce similar gyrations in others. You only have to go to HIMSS once to witness the similarities among top vendors.

2. *High barriers to entry*: Big, expensive enterprise inpatient EHRs are not easy to develop. Even if a new firm had a ready-to-ship product, it's incredibly hard to disrupt the incumbent's stronghold. The notoriously long sales and implementation cycles in healthcare (12-18 months) would starve most startups before they could reach profitability. Not to mention the high EHR substitution costs that are a perennial deterrent for customers. All these factors end up manifesting as reduced competition and higher prices.

3. *Product evolution*: Oligopolies can make competing products more homogenous (like steel and gas) or differentiated (like

cars and phones). The inpatient EHR market is going in the former direction. Most inpatient EHRs tend to have similar overall functionality and new features end up being available elsewhere eventually.

Oligopolies are not exclusive to Health IT; they exist in many markets. For example, take wireless (AT&T, Verizon, Sprint, T-Mobile), beverages (Coke, Pepsi), and airplanes (Boeing, Airbus). But the clusters of large firms in healthcare come with an important distinction. Compared to other industries, there is a strikingly disproportionate lack of consumer transparency and empowerment in healthcare. Consumerism may keep the oligarchs on their toes in other industries but because healthcare is almost a black box for the patients, oligopolies here are really regional monopolies. This is why it's a relatively safe prediction to say that the top 10 inpatient EHR vendor list won't change much in the next few years. The big will get even bigger.

One exception may be those companies that manage to have EHR offerings as a result of cross-subsidy from other lines of business, like GE and McKesson. Those are half-hearted attempts which will eventually die a natural death when the corporate establishment tags them as a distraction from the core money-making business. Siemens recently sold its EHR business to Cerner. GE has already made a public announcement of their intent to shut theirs down. Rumors point to McKesson being next on the chopping block.

The outpatient EHR market is significantly more fragmented with almost 760 vendors (compared to 179 inpatient EHR vendors) and new entrants trickling in frequently. Still, the vendor power seems to be concentrated with a few large firms. Top five vendors in the industry (Epic.com, Allscripts.com, eClinicalWorks.com, NextGen.com, GEHealthcare.com) again account for more than half market share. Top 10 vendors expand it to nearly 70% coverage.[7] This kind of distribution doesn't bode well for the remaining 750 or so vendors as a massive market consolidation is inevitable in the next five years. Ever-increasing regulatory requirements like Meaningful Use (more on that in the section 2.4. Policy) are hastening the demise of ineffective vendors.

There are two names that often appear to be outliers in the EHR world, distinct enough to warrant a closer look. First is VistA (www.ehealth.va.gov/VistA.asp), the Health IT system of the Veterans Affairs (VA) Department. A pioneer in electronic medical record-keeping, VistA is a mammoth system deployed universally across more than 1,500 sites and providing care to over 8 million veterans. In the VA microcosm, thousands of users get trained on the mandated home-grown system every year. Billions of dollars have been devoted to its much-deserved maintenance and evolution. But just like the lumbering giants of a forgotten era, VistA's extinction was inevitable. In July 2015, the Department of Defense awarded Cerner a $4.8 billion, 10-year contract for commercial replacement of VistA. Thankfully though, the more than 150 distinct applications and millions of lines of code of VistA may carry on through the Open Source Electronic Health Record Agent (OSEHRA.org).

The second outlier is Epic Systems of Verona, WI. Epic seems to have a culture different than that found at most Health IT vendors. Its hiring is skewed toward young, local graduates in the early stages of their careers. Employees get modest titles, and Epic's customers tend to behave like a devoted cult. The firm's HIMSS booth staff never seems to be pushy or overselling, and Epic is very careful about PR and making partner endorsements. I was once cautioned by an Epic interoperability team member to not mention Epic's name many times in a PR release, and instead focus on the customer's name.

Epic is a formidable player in Health IT and yields market-shaping power. If you are an entrepreneur in healthcare, there is a good chance that one day you'll be thinking about your product's interaction with Epic. My intention in outlining these characteristics is to help you make your own predictions around Epic's corporate behavior and future. Because of its dominating market share, Epic gets disproportionately dinged for interoperability (or rather, a perceived lack thereof). In reality, all vendors have the same interoperability challenges, not just Epic. Some, like Cerner and AthenaHealth, just do a better job keeping public perception favorable.

An interesting fact is that both VistA and Epic are written in the "M" programming language, also known as "Massachusetts General Hospital Utility Multi-Programming System," or MUMPS.

MUMPS was created in the late 1960s at Massachusetts General Hospital in Boston. Designed for manipulating massive databases, it was built with a metadata-driven approach, much like today's NoSQL. Aside from Epic and VistA, major healthcare industry players currently using MUMPS in some form are: Meditech.com, Allscripts.com, InterSystems.com, and QuestDiagnostics.com. It is popular in the financial industry as well. TD Ameritrade, the Bank of England, and Barclays Bank are all reputedly still running systems on MUMPS.

When tech professionals first learn about M's ongoing use in Health IT, they are puzzled as to why the largest systems in healthcare still run on an obscure programming language and database system from the 1960s. The reason is simple: it's cheaper and easier to keep going with what works than to rebuild everything from the ground up. Perhaps this explains why some systems in the financial industry are rumored to be still running on COBOL.

2.3. Health Information Exchanges

2.3.1. HIEs: What and Why

So far we have talked about EHRs, which were primarily born out of the need for digitizing the information *inside* a health organization. An EHR serves as the key information system that enables a hospital or clinic to take care of the patient within its boundaries. The effectiveness of such inward-focused systems decreases when care is transitioned over to an external entity. For example, when a patient relocates, changes insurance carriers, or is discharged to recover elsewhere, how does the new entity receiving the patient access previously created information? And for that matter, how does *any* care organization tap into medical information created outside their own system? That's where HIEs come in.

HIEs are the exchange hubs for the post-EHR era we are entering. They are created and governed by organizations that are typically in geographical proximity to each other. For example, the largest physician group and hospital network in a metropolitan area may get together to fund and operate a local HIE. This enables them to share critical information across the region and to consolidate some common business needs (like connecting to state immunization registries). The primary requirement of sharing information is why the operating keyword of HIEs is "interoperability."

The finance industry provides a good analogy for understanding the role of HIEs. Banks have internal information systems that help organize workforce, customer accounts, and transactions, but it's the Automated Clearinghouse (ACH) network that provides information exchange between banks.[8] The individual bank account holder is like the patient, their bank is like the hospital (or clinic), and ACH serves the HIE's purpose.

When it comes to patient information, HIEs enable an inter-organization vantage which I like to call the "Longitudinal Patient Record" (LPR). The LPR stores patient information that is spread *horizontally* across time, care settings, and organizations. It doesn't go as *vertically* deep into one visit's information as an EHR does. Its primary purpose is to serve as a lynchpin across multiple visits and disconnected organizations, providing a critical common denominator.

2.3.2. A Brief History of HIEs

While HIEs are not as old as EHRs, the concept of aggregating health information in a community still goes back a long way. The first explicit effort started in 1991 when the John A. Hartford Foundation of New York sponsored a "Community Health Management Information System" (CHMIS) in order to create a central database for sharing information between organizations in seven communities (six states - Washington, Iowa, Minnesota, New York, Vermont, Ohio and one metropolitan area - the city of Memphis). After years of searching for a self-sustaining business model, this initiative eventually ran out of funding. More initiatives were started in the mid-1990s, albeit under a new moniker: "Community Health Information Networks" (CHINs).[9] CHINs were funded commercially and used a transaction-based approach that avoided creating a central repository, thereby meeting the ownership needs of each participating organization. After initial enthusiasm and minor success, most CHIN initiatives ended in a stalemate of regional politics, misaligned incentives, and unwilling participants.

In the ensuing years, the terms "Health Information Exchange" and "Regional Health Information Organization" (RHIO) were used interchangeably to describe projects in this category. It is now widely accepted that *HIE* (the noun) is the right label for the underlying infrastructure of *health information exchange* (the verb), whereas RHIO refers to the actual governing body over HIEs. But like all new concepts in a rapidly evolving industry, the wires have been crossed many times and many places in the public dialogue about HIEs.

The golden age of federally-supported, inorganic HIEs was kicked off in 2004 when the Agency for Healthcare Quality and Research (AHRQ) funded $166 million in grants and contracts. This stimulus included State and Regional Demonstration (SRD) projects for supporting health information exchanges. Plush $5 million grants were awarded to six states: Indiana, Delaware, Rhode Island, Tennessee, Colorado, and Utah. This money followed the gravitational law of federal funding to end up in Health IT vendors' coffers.

Simultaneously, digitization of health information was starting to feel like yesterday's news. The overall Health IT market was beginning to have a "What's next?" moment. Shifting the dialogue to information exchange was becoming fashionable. The word "interoperability" started showing up in marketing pitches and in industry rhetoric. In fact, the HIMSS conference debuted a physical location called the "Interoperability Showcase" (interoperabilityshowcase.org) in 2005 to provide a staged demonstration of interoperability and standards-based connectivity across vendors. Ever since then the contrived exhibit has become a consistent feature forcing competing vendors to nervously mingle with each other every year.

HIEs also developed organically in several markets and academic settings where the geopolitical environment was conducive to regional participants uniting to create a cost-effective network for exchanging health information. For example, Inland Northwest Health Services (inhs.info) was founded in 1994 by two competing healthcare entities in Spokane, WA. HealthBridge.org (founded 1997 in Cincinnati, OH) and Indiana Health Information Exchange (ihie.org, founded 2004) were other examples of the rare HIEs that found business viability.

It turned out that propping up an industry-wide HIE market needed the government's visible hand. That support came in one fell swoop with the passing of the American Recovery and Reinvestment Act in 2009. Aside from the promethean move of incentivizing EHR adoption, the law allocated about $564 million for public HIE projects nationwide. As a result, by mid-2010, 50 states and 6 territories had received initial funds to begin planning for and establishing HIE programs. As always, the gravitational law of federal funding made this money flow to Health IT vendors. The ensuing public contracts resulted in upsizing of vendors like Axolotl.com, Relayhealth.com, and Medicity.com. Eventually, these little fishes got swallowed by bigger ones. For example, Aetna acquired Medicity (2010), UnitedHealth Group bought Axolotl (2010), and Siemens bought MobileMD (2011).

2.3.3. Private HIEs: Where the Future Is

Getting constant cooperation and cost-justification between competing providers has proven to be the Achilles' heel of most failed public HIEs. Private HIEs, typically owned by one or more hospital system(s), have proven more resistant to non-cooperation and political issues. Also known as "Enterprise HIEs," private HIEs aim to drive business to the sponsoring hospital system(s) in form of referrals and orders. Functionally, they cover the same features as the public HIEs but have differing priorities.

Private HIEs are one of the fastest-growing market segments because of the shift to accountable care. In 2010, the Affordable Care Act (discussed more in section 2.4. Policy) introduced new payment models that forced care organizations to be more involved over the long run and coordinate every aspect of patient care. Since then, organizations across the nation have been reshaping to become Accountable Care Organizations (ACOs) that have tighter affiliations and can service patient population needs completely. In other words, the move toward accountable care has spurred the emergence of private networks of healthcare organizations with a common financial incentive to optimize care. In order to do this effectively, ACOs need health information *exchange* (the verb, and hence, the noun) that can give a comprehensive picture of the network. This is what HIE software is designed to do. Despite all the gloom-and-doom analysis of why HIEs may fail, the future looks bright for the software vendors that are focused on private HIE opportunities.

2.3.4. HIE Market Characteristics

Interestingly, the two most notable characteristics of the HIE market have to do with what these exchanges lack, and not what they offer.

First is the peculiar lack of a viable business model. While notable exceptions do exist, most public HIEs were (and are) operated on grant-based funding. More often than not, the cost of building an HIE infrastructure and its governance is shared unequally. Unfortunately, not all participants contribute the same amount of time, money and resources. For example, a leading hospital system with major market share may lean in heavily, as compared to a smaller community hospital or group practice. This results in different definitions of acceptable ROI and levels of commitment among the HIE participants. Invigorated with federal funding, nearly all 50 state HIEs followed a "build it and they will come" strategy and partnered with vendors to create local public HIEs. In 2013, an estimated 280 public HIEs existed in the United States.[10] As initial funding fades out, most will likely close shop or become part of the state Medicaid funding, or be replaced by a network of viable private HIEs.

The second notable characteristic of the HIE market is the conspicuous lack of participation from insurance companies. Payers had almost nothing to do with public HIEs, and have stayed away from the private HIEs in the past. The latter trend is beginning to change as payers mingle with large IDNs to create regional ACO networks which require private HIEs to operate. Aetna and UnitedHealth Group's HIE software vendor acquisitions (Medicity and Axolotl, respectively) prove that.

There are some fundamental questions about how to manage the exchanges of information between competing providers. For example, patients frown on privacy and consent management misalignments between the different organizations they visit. Providers often falsely equate information sharing with patient sharing. Administrators worry about incorrect data usage and out-of-context interpretation. Although no one admits it publicly, the fact that information exchange makes it easier for patients to switch providers is unnerving to many. Healthcare is a business and thus turf wars are always simmering under the surface.

2.3.5. What About HIE Software from an EHR Vendor?

Admittedly, the separation between EHRs and HIEs is mostly theoretical. Big EHR companies claim to create de-facto HIEs by connecting multiple customer installations in a geographic area. Epic's "Care Everywhere" offering exemplifies this perfectly. Epic's customers tend to cluster together, giving the firm regional dominance in many places. Care Everywhere is essentially Epic's own way of hooking up multiple customer installations so that they can send and receive information to each other. Sounds like an HIE, doesn't it?

HIE platforms bred by EHR vendors have the advantage of an insider's perspective on the quantity and quality of the information being exchanged. They have the luxury of not having to deal with a wide variety of external systems, as they simply connect different implementations of the in-house EHR. Pure-play HIE platforms in the market (like Medicity.com and OrionHealth.com) are required to deal with more variation. For example, they need a much more robust Master Patient Index (MPI) which can match patients across widely varying data sources.

On the flip side, several HIE software vendors have created or partnered to offer EHR-like functionality. Their reason for doing so is to service the rare HIE participants without an established EHR (e.g. rural solo practitioners who get state subsidies for using an HIE).

In the end, the act of health information exchange is what is important, rather than the pedigree of the vendor that supplies the software behind it. An EHR vendor's HIE product would have a home-ground advantage in facilitating the exchange of information generated in their own systems, but may not perform well when external vendors are in the mix. Pure-play HIE vendor solutions are harder to implement, but more suitable for markets where multiple EHR vendors are powering HIE participants. Both factions enable health information exchange (the verb).

Market turf wars aside, fundamental differences between EHR and HIE value propositions justify their separation. They may be made by the same vendor or used by the same organization, but their value propositions are distinct enough to coexist separately. Sections 3. Electronic Health Records and 4. Health Information Exchanges will further explain the distinction.

2.4. Policy

If there is any single aspect that defines the challenges of working in healthcare, it's the byzantine maze of regulations that run through the system. Venture capitalists, entrepreneurs, and even healthcare insiders roll their eyes when this topic comes up. For any health information entrepreneur, the usual blockbuster regulatory topics are HIPAA and the FDA. Both have been around for a long time, with enough websites and guides dedicated to them, so I won't discuss them here.

Rather than creating a very comprehensive list of important regulations, let's focus on two newer rules that are shaping the Health IT landscape: Meaningful Use and the Affordable Care Act.

2.4.1. Meaningful Use

How it came about

In some sense, the halcyon age of Health IT started when President George W. Bush, in his State of the Union address in January 2004, made it a national goal to wire the U.S. healthcare system. Months later, the Office of the National Coordinator for Health Information Technology or ONC, (healthIT.gov), was born with a budget of $42 million.

In the next five years, that $42 million blossomed one thousand-fold in $30 billion, mostly due to the $787 billion stimulus package that came with the American Recovery and Reinvestment Act (ARRA) in 2009. ARRA directed health spending through the enactment of the carefully-named "Health Information Technology for Economic and Clinical Health", or HITECH Act. HITECH injected a healthy dose of $30 billion to help graft health information technology on the aging healthcare system.[11]

The money was to be allocated through a program of incentives to encourage adoption of information technology. But how would the government ensure doctors and hospitals didn't end up buying suboptimal technology just to qualify for federal aid? For that reason, an elaborate set of criteria were developed for both sellers and buyers of information technology, aptly called "Meaningful Use" or simply MU (pronounced "em-you" and not like the Greek letter μ).

What it is

In a loose comparison, Meaningful Use is like the 5-Star Safety Ratings program created by the National Highway Traffic Safety Administration (NHTSA), which sets a minimum bar for a more efficient and safer automobile market. It's not a perfect analogy because car drivers are not required to prove that they are using a 5-Star product in order to get federal handouts. Which is what makes Meaningful Use all that more interesting.

The Meaningful Use program was designed to be enforced in three stages:

- Stage 1, started in 2011, aimed at seeding data capture and sharing capabilities
- Stage 2, started in 2014, focused on advancing clinical processes using information technology

- Stage 3, currently expected in 2017, should put the spotlight on improved outcomes

Those who pass Stage 1 tests get the marketing label of "2011 Edition Certified."[12] Likewise, Stage 2 test survivors get "2014 Edition Certified."[13] A nice side-effect of all this regulatory burden is that a fantastic list of vendors and their certified product(s) is available as the "Certified Health IT Product List" (CHPL, for short). CHPL, or as insiders jokingly call it, "Chapel," is accessible to the public at chpl.healthit.gov.

Each stage of MU can be viewed from two perspectives: the EHR technology vendor's and the provider's (i.e. their customers). The vendor gets MU *Certification*,[14] and the customer (i.e. Provider or Hospital) completes MU *Attestation*.[15] Certification usually entails a broader scope than attestation because vendors need to pass *all* relevant criteria to be certified in a particular functional area. Customers are given mandatory and optional criteria (called "Core" and "Menu" respectively), so their focus is a subset of the vendor's. For example, under Stage 2 a customer would attest to completing a HIPAA compliance risk analysis; that's just one criterion. But a vendor completing a certification for privacy and security needs to address eight very specific testing criteria.

MU Stage 1 was greeted with minimal resistance as it didn't ask for much. But with MU Stage 2, things went awry. The granular, prescriptive nature of MU Stage 2, in which the government micromanaged features of software and clinical practice, made it very unpopular with the technology industry and healthcare lobby. As a result, there has been periodic backpedaling and meandering by the ONC to make political amends against the backlash. The MU program has become a continuously-evolving mass of convoluted requirements that get more cryptic as time passes. Consulting firms love it and providers are beginning to wonder if it's just easier to pay the penalties of sticking with paper. MU Stage 3 has faced strong, persistent headwinds from lobbyists and industry organizations. In late April 2016, CMS announced that MU requirements will be made much more flexible (read "weakened"). The MU program will be folded into another, bigger initiative called the Merit-Based Incentive Payment System (MIPS), starting January 1, 2017.

Regardless, the MU program has gotten the ball rolling on multiple fronts. Archaic care delivery organizations that were hitherto dragging their feet on digitization were jolted by MU into taking the first step. The wide variations among EHR vendors was forced to narrow as the low-performers withered away under the burden of MU certification. Some of the surviving EHR vendors would probably argue that MU compliance has come at the cost of innovation, but given what the industry has to show for past "innovation," that may be a price worth paying.

2.4.2. Affordable Care Act

Signed into law on March 23, 2010, the "Patient Protection and Affordable Care Act"—shortened to "Affordable Care Act" or ACA, and unofficially also called "Obamacare"—was perhaps the most far-reaching healthcare regulation in recent history. Irrespective of its political divisiveness and controversial future, the law has triggered a series of changes that are reshaping fundamentals of the healthcare market.

These changes are happening not just because the industry is attracted to the new era ushered in by Obamacare, but also because of the implicit desire to move away from the status quo. The fragmented, costly care delivery in our country makes most people receptive to the idea of a (read "any") new model. Of course we can debate if a new model is the right model, but no one will disagree that the old model is broken.

New incentives

For an entrepreneur, the single most important change from ACA is payment reform. The law aims to reduce healthcare costs by encouraging the formation of networks that can coordinate patient care, called "Accountable Care Organizations" (ACOs). Think of it in terms of the shopping experience at a big box retailer like Target or Costco. If these stores didn't aggregate a long list of household items, one would have to shop at various individual specialty stores for groceries, hardware, clothing, and other needs. The retailer and consumer both benefit from bringing together many different items under one roof.

Similarly, ACOs assemble the usual parts of a care delivery system for the patient, everything from emergency room care, urgent care, hospitals, clinics, pharmacies, long-term care, home health care, primary care, to specialist care. This ensures that all needed care services are dovetailed in a low-cost, high-quality manner. ACOs make all providers jointly accountable for the health of their patients, encouraging cooperation amongst otherwise competing factions and ultimately saving money by avoiding unnecessary costs like redundant tests and procedures.

But the real disruption of an ACO, business-wise, is in the financial incentives that the organization gives its care providers. Traditionally, care providers have been paid for each service rendered, each physical exam, test, or procedure. This model is called "Fee for Service" (FFS), which can drive up costs, because it rewards providers for doing more, irrespective of need. FFS amounts to a zero-sum game between providers and payers: one loses money, the other gains it.

ACOs still do FFS, but they are also authorized to create additional incentives for keeping costs down. Participating providers in an ACO become eligible for bonuses when they demonstrate that quality care has been delivered more efficiently to a population within their network. The challenge is that becoming an ACO requires significant investment (like hiring care managers and buying analytics software), and if they don't end up saving money, someone has to foot the bill. Not to mention that just one or two high-cost episodes with a patient can blow an ACO's budget for that individual. With those caveats in mind, consider some high-level examples of an ACO's alternative payment arrangements:

1. *Modified Fee-for-service*:

   - One-sided: The providers are paid a portion of the ACO's savings, and not penalized for going above the cost target, so there is no downside risk for providers.

   - Two-sided: Savings are shared more generously with providers, but penalties also exist.

2. *Bundled Payments*: Providers take the maximum financial risk, as they contract for a single payment for all the services that may be rendered. This fixed payment may be based on a disease episode (e.g. hip replacement) or time-based (e.g. monthly, annual). Essentially providers need to project, monitor and manage costs like a payer, because increasing utilization mean less profit.

ACO creation and bundled payments are part of an ongoing shift in the public and private payer strategy to drive improvements in quality while slowing growth in spending. This new demand-side strategy has been labeled "Value Based Purchasing" (VBP). VBP programs adjust insurance payments to reward hospitals based on the quality of care provided. Federal authorities started testing VBP models a decade ago when the "Deficit Reduction Act" of 2005 authorized CMS to implement a new *Pay-for-Performance* (P4P) Program for Medicare services. P4P was perhaps the first demonstration of VBP by a public payer. ACOs are the latest.

Impact on technology

Current estimates point to more than 782 ACOs serving around 23 million Americans.[16] All that growth has come in the last four years, with organizations aggressively expanding their reach and scope to form comprehensive delivery systems that can manage a patient population across all care settings. The real tangible turning point came in January 2015, when CMS announced a goal of tying 50% of their payments to VBP models by end of 2018. That one announcement on its own was enough to make 2015 a landmark year for healthcare transformation. It was the first time that there was clear commitment to VBP and timeline for adoption proposed by the largest payer in the country.

All this massive restructuring and realignment have kicked off some clear technology consumption trends. Notably:

- As healthcare systems acquire or partner to expand, the need for information integration and exchange increases. This bodes well for technologies that are facilitating communication and enhancing information transport.

- The new hospital system will care tremendously about helping patients avoid visits to the ER or clinics. If fewer patients utilize their services, the organization retains more of its money. Patient engagement tools and services like mobile self-care apps and televisits will be in high demand.

- Because providers get paid more for keeping their patients healthy and out of the hospital, there will be an intense focus on prevention and chronic disease management (a.k.a. "Care Management") that meets certain quality benchmarks. Demand for technologies and programs that help deliver these preventive and care management services will be high.

- Doctors and hospitals in an ACO arrangement will be highly likely to refer patients to providers within the ACO network, because any external treatment is harder to track and usually more expensive. Solutions that make in-network referrals easy to send, monitor, and analyze will become important.

- Traditional insurance companies, having lost their grip on medical underwriting, will try to reinvent themselves. Some, like UnitedHealth Group and Aetna, have already made bold moves outside of insurance. Others will buy or partner with provider organizations to serve the 40 million or so previously-uninsured individuals that have entered the healthcare system due to Obamacare.

Changes in the ecosystem

Gazing into my crystal ball, I see that the mad rush toward the ACO model will yield mediocre results when the primary driving organization is a hospital system. That is because big hospitals are most likely going to use the ACO transformation as an excuse to merge, acquire, and gain market share. And as they merge with competitors and purchase physician practices, the fundamental cost reduction only comes from scale (to negotiate with payers, employers) and never from efficiency. So it always ends up being a temporary fix.

The successful stories will come from smaller, physician-driven ACOs, which typically focus on a specialty. The fields of orthopedics and nephrology are already showing a successful transition to this model. Physician groups can lower costs by keeping patients out of the hospital and taking care of them upfront. Hospital-led ACOs tend to focus on cost-effective management of patients once they are admitted. Further, specialty groups have dedicated expertise for certain diseases and can hone in on the best practices for those conditions more effectively than one-stop-shop hospital systems. For example, nephrologists know how to optimize dialysis care for End-Stage Renal Disease (ESRD), orthopedic surgeons know degenerative joint diseases, cardiologists manage congestive heart failure, and so on. The dual goal of making care cheaper and higher-quality is more likely to be achieved when the executing team is focused and the problem set is narrow.

Obamacare also brings some striking changes to the payer ecosystem. From an entrepreneur's perspective, the two to note are new Medical Loss Ratio (MLR) rules and changes to medical underwriting.

Insurance companies can classify their expenses in two major categories: administrative and non-administrative. The latter applies to activities that directly affect patient care, like reimbursing claims and running quality improvement initiatives. Administrative expenses are everything else, like marketing, salaries, provider contracting, and bonuses.

Under the new MLR rules, large group plans (more than 100 insured) must spend at least 85% of their premiums on non-administrative functions (80% for small group plans). They must also publicly report the portion of premium dollars spent on these non-administrative activities in each state where they operate. That requirement incentivizes payers to adopt technologies that can make it cheaper to do administrative functions, especially around managing a provider network. That's good news for startups because now they have a shot at getting the attention of such orthodox organizations. For example, if a startup can make physician credentialing more efficient, it will get noticed, as that's one of the most expensive aspects of administering an insurance plan.

The other major change is in medical underwriting. Before Obamacare, applying for a health insurance policy meant that the applicant had to disclose existing health conditions, previous medical and surgical history, ongoing treatments, and possibly undergo a checkup. That intrusive process was purely for the benefit of the insurance company which would use the resulting information to adjust monthly premiums, and figure out coverage, exclusions, and limits. Additionally, companies could have whimsical variations in their proprietary underwriting rules across geographies. That deplorable era of medical underwriting ended on January 1, 2014 when the "Guaranteed Issue" part of Obamacare came into effect. That made it illegal for insurance companies to ask for the applicant's medical history and adjust prices according to it. Now, only four factors are permitted to be the basis of premium calculations: age, tobacco use, geographic area and individual vs. family status. To a conventional insurance company, these restrictions surely feel like driving blind, which may explain why insurance premium rates went up across the industry.

The overall effect should be net positive. Now that insurers can't conveniently skew membership toward healthy individuals, they are actually sharing the risk with the insured. This means they are always looking for new ways to predict claims and the risk of the population that they are obliged to serve. It's a massive shift in incentives that makes conventional giants more open to new ideas.

3

Electronic Health Records

3.1. Anatomy of an EHR

3.1.1. What Makes a Typical EHR?

That's a loaded question, especially because the field changes frequently and boundaries are constantly shifting. EHRs can be examined in functional chunks called "modules." At a high level, these modules can be classified into two categories:

1. *Clinical Modules:* These tackle everything related to the actual activities of caring for a patient. For example: Documentation (where a clinician would record their notes), Order Entry (where a clinician would prescribe medications), and Results Reporting (where a clinician would access lab test results). Basically, these modules handle the daily shift-based workflows of clinicians and caregivers.

2. *Administrative Modules:* Like all businesses, healthcare needs recording tools for the practical realities of commerce. Enterprise Billing, Appointment Scheduling, and Workforce Management are all examples of such administrative modules.

The above categorization comes from a functional point of view, but usage depends on the user's context. For EHRs, the two major contexts are the inpatient and outpatient care settings.

1. *Outpatient:* This pertains to the suite of functionality that serves a typical clinic, locations with services that don't require overnight stays and treat less complex cases. Your neighborhood primary care physician or pediatrician office

is a good example. These settings mostly need software modules for tasks like scheduling, lab ordering, and prescriptions.

2. *Inpatient:* This suite of functionality serves the typical workflows of a hospital department like the Emergency Room, Labor & Delivery Suite, or the Operating Room. As you can imagine, inpatient procedures are typically more complex, with heavy billing and convoluted workflow. Module-wise, they require functionality for clinical documentation, billing, and procedure notes, among other things.

It's important to note that there is a huge functional overlap between inpatient and outpatient EHRs. Both settings require billing and clinical documentation, for example, but the functional scope and priorities are usually different.

The remainder of this section describes the least common denominator of EHR functionality at the highest level of detail. It's hard to nail down a comprehensive (or indisputable) feature list of EHRs because they are constantly evolving. With that caveat out of the way, here is a framework for thinking about EHR fundamentals, each addressed in a subsequent subsection:

1. EHRs help with billing - that's "Revenue Cycle Management" (RCM).

2. EHRs let clinicians and staff record data about care - that's "Documentation."

3. EHRs enable physicians to prescribe - that's "Computerized Provider Order Entry" (CPOE).

4. EHRs can digitize day-to-day operational logistics, specially for clinics and outpatient facilities - that's "Practice Management" (PM).

5. EHRs can let patients view their own data - that comes under the "Personal Health Record" (PHR).

6. EHRs can serve as the information system for various departments of a hospital. Each specialized adaptation becomes a particular "Departmental System."

3.1.2. Best-of-Breed vs. Integrated: The Eternal Struggle

The digitization of health didn't start with an end-vision of an enterprise system. At first, small groups of innovators with a common interest got together to create better workflows using computers. That's why early attempts created "Best-of-Breed" systems that focused on a particular niche like radiology, billing, and anesthesiology.

The importance of integrated enterprise EHRs is beyond question, though. In the last two decades they have found firm footing in healthcare, and made some vendors into billionaires.[17] The best integrated EHRs deliver all-encompassing suites that combine the value propositions of multiple best-of-breed systems and reducing integration issues. Practically speaking it's simpler for large customers to buy from a single reputable vendor. The risk-averse purchasers' saying "Nobody ever got fired for buying IBM equipment" applies to healthcare too.

One can argue that the pendulum keeps swinging slowly between the popularity of vendors with the wholesale enterprise-suite approach and niche vendors with a more retail-oriented best-of-breed approach. The appeal of one-size-fits-all enterprise systems seems to have reached its peak recently. This preference may linger for a while due to regulatory cash infusions, but the market appetite for tailored, smaller solutions is going up.

Pick up industry newsletters Rock Health or Health 2.0 and you'll see funding and execution progress for new, narrower-than-EHR value propositions. The next decade will see non-EHR startups change the status quo for many issues in healthcare. Some examples worth noting are: OmadaHealth.com (digitally-enhanced care management programs), Flatiron.com (oncology information technology), Ayasdi.com (sophisticated data analytics), Kyruus.com (demand and provider capacity optimization), and EvolentHealth.com (consulting and care management outsourcing company that went public mid-2015).

Of course, some of the focused startups of today will get bigger and transform into the enterprise behemoths of tomorrow. It's a cycle, after all.

3.2. Revenue Cycle Management

3.2.1. The Crucial Role of Revenue

More efficient billing was one of the main reasons why IT was first adopted in healthcare. Revenue Cycle Management (RCM) focuses on inpatient billing and has become a mature field in the last 15 years. In the early 2000s, big hospital systems were moving away from paper-based billing and investing in centralized, digital financial systems. In fact, early CIO (Chief Information Officer) positions often reported to CFOs (Chief Financial Officers) and not CEOs, as is the norm today.

RCM software's central value proposition is about increasing the amount of revenue collected. It is needed because the process of submitting claim information and receiving payment is mind-numbingly complex. Many variables exist: a plethora of insurance companies, changing reimbursement rules for each insurer, different copay requirements, retroactive eligibility, claim rejections for unclear reasons, and back-and-forth clarifications. It's a cat-and-mouse game that only leads to more costs. Given that the operating margins for most not-for-profit hospitals is in the 0–4% range, there is a need for software that can help navigate these processes and improve returns. That's RCM.

The traditional framework for RCM technology divides it into three categories:

1. *Front-end Work:* Crass as it may seem, the revenue collection process starts when the patient initiates contact with the

organization. Workflows included in this category are the ones that happen before the patient receives actual care services. For example: appointment scheduling, registration, collecting patient demographic and insurance information, insurance verification, and getting pre-authorization.

2. *Mid-cycle Work:* This is where actual clinical practice meets billing. The key objectives are managing the clinical practice within established guidelines, capturing charges correctly, enabling complete clinical documentation, and ensuring accurate codification into claims. Mid-cycle also includes case management functionality that helps coordinate events (admissions, discharges, and follow-ups), and then optimizes these events for claim submission to insurers. Another interesting functionality relates to a file called "Charge Description Master" (CDM, or simply "Chargemaster") which is a comprehensive list of all the billable items in a hospital. System tools for CDM maintenance, updates, cross-reference and research are found in mid-cycle RCM software. It's also worth noting that the term "Health Information Management" (HIM) refers to the codification of documented clinical care and patient conditions to support billing claims.

3. *Back-end Work:* These functions are similar to most business back offices and accounting departments. For example: claims submission, processing and payment posting, denials management, follow-up, customer service, refunds/adjustments, and collections.

There are several big trends impacting the world of healthcare finance and RCM technology. One has to do with how bills are created and another with how they are paid.

3.2.2. Trend: Billing Explosion

Healthcare billing is dominated by a system called ICD (International Classification of Diseases) that is used to codify bills and release payments. Currently in the U.S. the widely-used version is ICD-9, which was developed nearly 30 years ago. The World Health Organization adopted ICD-10 as the international version in 1990. Eighteen years later, in 2008, the U.S. government first declared its intention of going live with it. The announcement was followed by industry backlash and the ensuing lobbying managed to keep pushing back the switch until everyone got tired of predicting when the ICD-10 transition might actually happen.

The mandate to begin coding in ICD-10 finally came to pass on October 1, 2015, after widespread frantic preparation and doomsday scenarios reminiscent of Y2K. Overnight, the number of official billing codes increased five-fold; from roughly 14,000 in ICD-9 to 69,000 in ICD-10.

Think about what that means for startups. Billing in healthcare just got spectacularly more granular (read "complex"). Insurers can now demand more detailed claims and have an unprecedented ability to zoom in on what care has been delivered. Doctors and nurses now need to better document conditions and their treatments so that medical coders can pinpoint them with higher fidelity.

The situation is like a neighborhood grocery store being asked to deal with a Walmart-like number of SKUs. Scaling up to this new level of detail can't be accomplished merely by employee re-training and procedural changes. It requires new technology tools that enable organizations to adapt to this new, hyper-detailed view of the care delivery world. Startups that can use machine learning to increase medical coder productivity or create intelligent user interfaces that make required data entry easier for clinicians would be welcomed.

3.2.3. Trend: Surging Deductibles

For the past decade, insurance plans with deductibles have been growing in adoption. More interestingly, the size of deductibles has skyrocketed. A 2015 survey by the Kaiser Family Foundation found that 81% of plans offered deductibles and the average deductible was $1,077.[18] That's more than a threefold increase from $303 in 2006, and several times more than growth in wages over the same period. With Obamacare's individual mandate pushing everyone to be insured, buyers are choosing high-deductible plans simply because they have lower premiums.

For a patient, the deductible comes out-of-pocket and gets treated in the same possessive manner as personal cash. This results in retail-like behavior where patients shop around for the best deal, either in terms of convenience or cost. The rise in lower-premium, higher deductible plans also increases delinquencies because many who buy on public insurance exchanges are individuals with poor cash-flow situations, unable to fulfill large deductibles.

All these changes mean that retail technologies around consumer behavior, credit profiles, and billing are now ripe for application in healthcare. Doctor's offices and hospitals now need to collect money from individuals and thus risk getting paid late or not at all. They have a real need to instill patient loyalty and satisfaction by providing a smooth billing experience.

This means good times for companies that can create price-transparent marketplaces, help patients compare services, create easy-to-understand bills, predict credit risk for providers, and help with payment reminders and collection. The financial fundamentals of consumerism have finally arrived in healthcare.

3.3. Documentation

Documentation in EHRs refers to the notes that a clinical professional creates in the course of delivering care. Beyond the idealistic purpose of knowledge transfer between caregivers, documentation serves as the formal proof for reimbursement and a substrate for reporting on quality measures. Words contained in (or missing from) a clinical document decide how much a clinician gets paid or who wins a malpractice lawsuit.

The design, content, and user interaction of these notes changes depending on the care setting. Documenting in the Operating Room, the Emergency Room, the Intensive Care Unit, and the Outpatient Clinic all have their unique needs. Having said that, there is a set of three common documentation structures that are used everywhere: Forms, Flowsheets, and Notes.

3.3.1. Forms

Self-explanatory, in a way. EHR forms are essentially electronic versions of the paper forms that one would find in a care delivery workflow, like the History & Physical (H&P) Form, and the Triage Form. The easiest way to understand their format is to compare them with Microsoft Word. The basic design has multiple data-input fields, categorized as sections/subsections and vertical scrolling. For example, an H&P Form in an EHR would have a section called "Family History" which would have checkboxes for diseases like diabetes, high blood pressure, and asthma. A section named "Allergies" would allow a user to select an allergy and record details like start/stop date, and reaction. And so on.

Regrettably, most vendors choose to design forms in a way that doesn't always take advantage of the endless possibilities of an electronic user interface. EHR forms are usually created to mimic paper forms. Data input areas and their hierarchical sub-fields are a mind-numbing combination of *structured* data input widgets like drop-downs, radio-buttons, check-boxes, and date-pickers. That's where the curse of data entry begins.

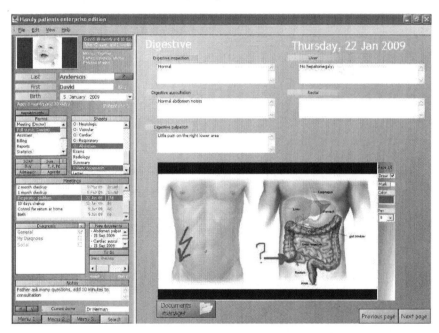

Screenshot of an EHR Documentation Form

(Image Credit: Wikipedia User DaCarpenther, Source: Oguntoye EMR)

3.3.2. Flowsheets

These are almost exclusively used for nursing documentation. Nursing workflow tends to involve repeated tedious tasks and multiple handoffs. For example, three shifts of nursing staff could be giving medications every 4 hours, changing wound dressings twice daily, or taking vitals every hour in the Intensive Care Unit (ICU). This is why flowsheets are structured like Microsoft Excel, with time-based columns that are crossed horizontally by documentation rows (or vice versa).

Don't expect Excel-like logical transformations for data, though. No pivot tables here. The fanciest functionality available is usually minor manipulations like:

- *Grouping*: Often rows are grouped together under a category-title row. For example, a "Vitals" parent row will have the heart rate, blood pressure, and pulse rows under it.

- *Totals*: Some of the repeated documentation in nursing care keeps track of a particular parameter, like fluid totals for cardiac patients. How much was given as intravenous infusion or as oral fluid vs. how much was observed in the urinary drainage bag? Some rows are pre-configured to do those calculations.

- *Graphs*: Where there are calculations, there is a chance to display some simple graphs. In conventional EHRs these tend to be preset to certain rows and not really available for ad-hoc graphing.

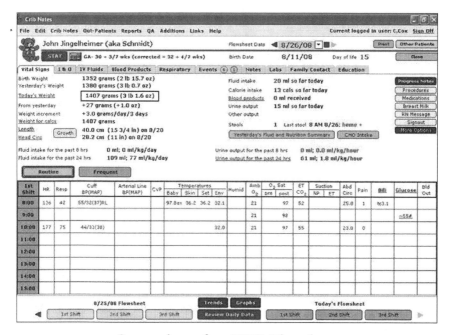

Screenshot of an EHR Flowsheet

(Image Credit and Copyright: Grand Rounds Software, LLC. Reproduced with permission.)

3.3.3. Notes

There are documentation use cases where a clinical user is looking to quickly record a standard interaction with a patient. Usually this is done in a boilerplate way, with only a few tweaks to a templated script. For example, recording a procedure note for fluoroscopy may look like this:

"PROCEDURE IN DETAIL:

After an appropriate written consent was obtained, the patient was brought to the fluoroscopy room and put into the prone position. The low back was aseptically prepped with alcohol x3 and draped in a sterile fashion. Under fluoroscopic guidance, the left L4-L5 facet joints were identified. A 22-gauge, 3 1/2 inch needle was inserted and directed under fluoroscopy into the left L4-L5 facet. Once the joint space was entered as confirmed by fluoroscopy, a solution containing 3 cc of .25% Bupivicaine and 2 cc DepoMedrol was injected. The needle was withdrawn intact.

A similar procedure was also done at the right L5-S1 facet joints under fluoroscopic guidance. The patient tolerated the procedure very well without any complications.

DISPOSITION: The patient was observed for additional 10 minutes before discharge.

PLAN: _____ "

Most of the content above is essentially a pre-configured template with the underlined parts written to fit a particular patient's procedure. EHRs have collections of these frequently-used templates that are either usually part of the shipping product's content library or are created by the implementation team as a part of the go-live for a clinical facility. Often there are keyboard shortcuts (like the tab key) that help users jump from one data-entry point to another.

3.3.4. The Data Entry Curse

It might take more than 40 clicks to note that a patient has a family history of mitral valve prolapse in an electronic H&P form. Contrast that with a one-line scribble on paper that takes a few seconds. Clinicians using such EHRs rightfully complain that they are spending less time with patients and more time doing data entry.

The real silent killer of user interface atrocities is the *unstructured* free-text field. For developers, it's easy to sprinkle free text fields in the user experience. For users, it provides the vain satisfaction of literary freedom. They can quickly type the terse lingo that the medical field is famous for and get on with their day, but such freedom is devastating from a machine's perspective. Free text is hard to interpret semantically. For example, how many variations of the term "Myocardial Infarction" exist? "AMI," "MI," "Heart Attack" ... more than you think!

Natural Language Processing (NLP) enthusiasts argue that such issues are going to be moot in the future. I agree, in principle. If IBM Watson is available to sift through the endless permutations and combinations of human brevity, slang, and abject errors, then perhaps we needn't worry about what we are typing into text fields. Allowing for natural language has already happened with Google searches and auto-correct on word processors, so why not with medical data entry?

Why not, indeed. But until that future arrives, I think we need a more pragmatic strategy, and that means creating better user interfaces. EHRs are probably not the only software that forces time-constrained, highly-paid professionals to input content for a commercial transaction. Creating beautiful, engaging user experiences is both a science and art. We need more arbitrage and diffusion from non-medical fields. There are content management paradigms yet unexplored in EHRs (like wikis and blogging platforms). The use of gesture-based, touch input is rare too. Perhaps EHR input can be augmented by real-time speech recognition, already a relatively mature technology. More on that later in the book.

An interesting side effect of cumbersome user interfaces is the emergence of a new cottage industry on the outskirts of Health IT, called "Medical Scribes." These are hired hands who do nothing but take the physician's narrative and punch the keys on the keyboard to get that narrative into the EHR. Some may see this development as progress, but my view is contrarian. Instead of either training users better or mounting pressure on vendors to create better interfaces, introducing scribes seems like a knee-jerk expansion that adds cost to the overall system. Regrettably, the position of our industry behemoth American Medical Association on the use of scribes seems to be full of fascinated enthusiasm.[19]

3.3.5. Templates: Friend or Foe?

Template-based documentation has its supporters, who frame the benefits in terms of time-saving and standardization. Indeed, there are always super-users of EHRs who have the keystrokes down to a level of efficiency that makes documentation go fast. But there is another school of thought that views these hyper-scripted ways of medico-legal documentation as detrimental to the genuine practice of medicine.

If all it takes is a few simple keystrokes to generate an official recording of a laundry list of items, we risk losing its connection to the actual act of delivering care in real life. EHR design seems to favor generating better bills over better records. In fact, a December 2013 report by the Office of Inspector General (OIG) concluded that EHR documentation has made it easier to commit fraud.[20] The report implicated the two common EHR documentation practices:

1. *Copy-and-paste:* When a healthcare provider copies and pastes information from a patient's record multiple times, usually failing to update the data or ensuring its accuracy and ongoing applicability.

2. *Over-documentation:* When a user adds false or irrelevant documentation in order to create support for billing higher-level services.

I don't have a strong opinion about templates, either for or against. Be it electronic or on paper, we have always needed documentation in healthcare. Preventing quick documentation seems like a superficial way of fighting fraud. We should attack the root cause of fraud (financial incentives) instead.

3.3.6. Making Documentation Easier

Some EHRs also provide an interesting feature related to templates in the form of small macros that auto-expand into larger texts (Epic calls these "SmartPhrases"). Users can type a special key (like ".") to evoke a list of choices that get narrowed as the user types more characters. Once selected, the choice expands into the pre-formatted phrase or statement(s).

For example. ".abdomen" (or shorter ".abd") may turn into "Abdomen: Soft, non tender, no hepatosplenomegaly. Normal bowel sounds. No bruit." Or ".back" may expand into:

"- Inspection: Normal. No lordosis, kyphosis, scoliosis. Full range of movement. No discomfort.

- Stork test (pain in the affected region during single-leg hyperextension): pain.

- Palpation: No tightness, spasm, trigger points, tenderness.

- Pulses: Good dorsal pedis, posterior tibial pulses. No radio-femoral delay.

- Straight leg raising: Sitting negative. Supine negative.

- Patrick sign / Faber test: Negative.

- Sensation to light touch: Normal.

- Tone: Normal.

- Reflex: 2/4 right equals left. Plantar down going.

- Motor: 5/5 right equals left. Hoover negative.

- Gait: Normal"

The expanded text often has placeholder characters (like "*****" or "_____") scattered here and there to point to places which can be customized to the given patient. Epic's library of SmartPhrases is generally open to submissions, and users can also browse and select from other users' macros.

SmartPhrases are essentially user-generated mini-templates for documentation. There are some questions about their ability to scale gracefully under an increasing number of eager users. Personalization ability is good in the beginning, when the template library is lean and consistent. But as time passes and a user base grows, variation starts taking a toll. Pretty soon ".abdomen" has variations across users and departments (think ".abdomen-drjohn," ".abdomen-surgery," and ".abdomen-ER"). People then start complaining about how inefficient SmartPhrases are because they can't find the right one quickly anymore.

Data entry shortcuts are a good idea, but they need to be managed and administered in a central way, or curated by a group of authorized editors in a Wikipedia-like fashion.

There are other ways to ease documentation pain. Medical transcription already exists as a legitimate industry. Speech recognition and gesture-based input are some technology trends that are slowly gaining traction. More about them in section 5. Emerging Areas.

3.3.7. Administering Documentation

All the data entry structures described in this section are not turn-key value propositions. They need constant tweaking to be shaped in the right way for the culture and workflow of a given user community. That requires an administrative backend that select users (system administrators and IT staff typically) can use to make the needed changes.

Administration Modules include features that help in looking after the library of templates for forms, flowsheets, or notes that come with the EHR. They allow creating, copying, editing, publishing and deleting templates. Meta-configurations like connecting a template to an existing report, or restricting visibility of a template to certain users, are usually also possible.

with a different vendor's enterprise EHR. Health IT is not that interoperable (yet).

Clinical Decision Support

This is the *pièce de résistance* functionality of the CPOE system. To understand it, let's define Clinical Decision Support Systems (CDSS), a beloved concept in Medical Informatics.

A decision is when someone chooses between alternatives. Simply put, CDSS is a set of features that support health professionals in making the correct clinical decisions. CPOE is the poster child use case for a CDSS, further distinguished by the fact that physicians are the sole users of CPOE.

The CDSS part of a CPOE system generates alerts during an ordering session to notify of potential errors like contraindicated medications, duplicate orders, drug-drug interactions, and conflicting allergies. Aside from simply helping avoid mistakes, such alerts also enhance the accuracy of the right decisions. Examples include renal- and weight-based dose calculation, access to the clinical reference information, and substitute medication and test recommendations based on cost or coverage.

As you can probably imagine, these systems are dependent on up-to-date clinical evidence and guidelines. That knowledge base is provided by specialized vendors employing teams of clinicians who regularly sift through emerging clinical literature to elicit the latest best practices in clinical care. Well-known names in this trade are- ZynxHealth.com (owned by Hearst), ProvationMedical.com (owned by Wolters Kluwer), and Micromedex.com (owned by Thomson Reuters).

3.4.2. CPOE Usage

The jury is still out on CPOE efficacy, a favorite divisive topic for medical informatics researchers for decades. Some academic papers have shown a significant reduction in adverse events like drug over/under dose, interval errors, and harmful drug interactions after CPOE implementation. Others claim increased errors after implementation, like prescribing errors where clinicians choose the wrong drug or dose from a pull-down menu, write the prescription for the wrong patient, or enter duplicate orders.

While partisan arguments are inevitable for any new technology in healthcare, CPOE is the crown jewel of physician resistance to EHRs. You will probably never find a physician that loves her CPOE system. Reactions range from disinterested numbness at best, and vengeful hatred at worst. Older physicians are continuously appalled by tedious CPOE clicks, contrasting the laborious tasks with easy scribbles on paper forms or verbal-only orders of yesteryear. Younger physicians may not reminisce about paper workflows, but are also acutely aware of CPOE's inferior user experience, especially when consumer technology applications (like Google and Facebook) keep raising the bar.

Why is CPOE user experience so mediocre across vendors? Here are some key reasons:

- Vendors in this space are notorious for holding onto old technology stacks, which makes it harder to create modern software features.

- The burdensome mandate of regulations around prescriptions (like those around narcotics) makes CPOE requirements rigid.

- There is an inordinate amount of customer demand for customization of enterprise systems which spawns unmanageable variations, making it harder to upgrade consistently.

- The inherent evolving nature of medicine creates rapid change in underlying clinical content for CPOE which makes maintenance a more time- and resource-intensive task than usual.

- Organizations are stolid and slow on innovation in general.

The core, and somewhat humbling, reason behind unsatisfying CPOE experience is that medical orders are inherently complex and highly scrutinized workflows. Translating such mission-critical tasks into an efficient digital experience can't be a turn-key project, especially because healthcare organizations (and individual users) have natural variations in how they operate. That's why well-intentioned CDSS logic in CPOE ends up creating "alert exhaustion" for users; what should be considered helpful ends up being distracting.

Regardless, CPOE's potential for eliminating certain aspects of human error in physician orders is undeniable. Like all enterprise Health IT products, the important fact to remember is that CPOE is not just a technology, but an organizational commitment to redesigning processes and user workflows.

3.4.3. eMedication Administration Record

Although it may sometimes exist as a separate module, the Electronic Medication Administration Record (or eMAR) is an inseparable part of the clinical order workflow and hence a logical extension of CPOE. eMAR does what the name says: serves as the legal record of what drugs are given to a patient at the point of care. The user interface varies from vendor to vendor, but the information captured is in the same two categories: about the patient (like demographics or allergies) and about the prescription (like drug, dose, route, frequency, or site).

A notable instance of eMAR workflow is the use of assistive technologies like barcodes and RFID to enable real-world verifications at the bedside. In fact, the specific method of pairing the eMAR with item-level identification using barcodes has been called BCMA (Bar-coded Medication Administration) and has inspired several research studies. A sample workflow would look like the following: 1) Nurse scans their own ID badge to access eMAR, 2) Nurse scans the medication barcodes, 3) Nurse scans patient's ID wristband barcode, and finally 4) Nurse gives the patient her medications and 5) Nurse finalizes documentation in the eMAR.

It is estimated that on average a hospitalized patient is exposed to at least one medication administration error per day.[22] eMAR and associated technologies help organizations comply with the sacred mantra of medication administration—the "Five Rights"—the right medication, given to the right patient, in the right dose, by the right route, and at the right time.

3.4.4. ePrescribing

ePrescribing (or eRx) is the workflow of generating an electronic prescription and transmitting it through a special network to the information systems of insurers and dispensing pharmacies. In other words, eRx is what connects your prescribing physician's CPOE module to the neighborhood dispensing pharmacy (like CVS Caremark or Walgreens) By eliminating paper, eRx process helps to prevent the main reasons for prescription errors like the famously illegible physician hand-writing, incorrect dosing, duplicate medications, and missed allergic reactions.

How eRx came about is an interesting story. In 2001, the three largest Pharmacy Benefit Management (PBM) companies in the nation—CVS Caremark Corp., Express Scripts Inc., and Medco Health Solutions, Inc.—combined forces to create an entity called RxHub LLC that would facilitate information exchange between insurers and prescribing physicians. That same year, the National Association of Chain Drug Stores (NACDS) and the National Community Pharmacists Association (NCPA) joined hands to create a similar entity, (named "Surescripts") for connecting pharmacies with prescribing physicians. Eventually in 2008, the two merged under the surviving name of Surescripts.

Today the behemoth Surescripts network is used by more than 1,000 hospitals and handles information for more than 270 million insured lives. It processes more than 6 billion transactions each year, including nearly 700 million medication histories and more than 1 billion e-prescriptions. No wonder that many insiders think of Surescripts as the de facto national health information exchange network.

Sadly, not all of Surescripts' colossal success can be attributed to its own business execution. Federal regulation has been continuously pushing for eRx adoption, starting with the "Medicare Improvements for Patients and Providers Act" (MIPPA) of 2008, which authorized an eRx incentive program that lasted from 2009 to 2013. The push continued with the Meaningful Use program, which has had explicit requirements for using eRx technologies. No wonder that the percentage of office-based physicians using eRx has gone from 7% (December 2008) to 70% (April 2014) in less than six years.[23]

And all that federally-mandated traffic has zoomed back-and-forth across only one network, with the network operator charging for every transmission. The only prescription routing that Surescripts doesn't do belongs to closed systems like Kaiser Permanente. As well-intentioned as it may be, Surescripts is a prominent example of a government-created monopoly in healthcare. It's baffling why the eRx giant hasn't raised any antitrust concerns to date.

3.5. Practice Management

Practice Management (PM) systems help run the business functions of outpatient healthcare organizations. For a typical small or mid-sized doctor's office, this includes features like patient appointment scheduling, filing the insurance claims, handling accounting, etc. It is categorically *not* used as the EHR system or by the clinician. Instead, the main user is the office manager or front-desk staff.

A PM system relies on integration with an existing EHR for clinical documentation. All outpatient software vendors end up offering both EHR and PM systems because they need to be together for either of them to function properly. Here are the four high-level functional categories of a PM system:

Scheduling

The key day-to-day operation at most clinics and offices is managing patient appointments. It may appear that a simple Google or Outlook calendar could do the job, but handling the logistics of multiple service providers and giving patients flexible options behooves a robust tool, especially after you layer the basic logistics with automated workflow requirements (like canceled appointments, or needed equipment/personnel), managing several office locations, respecting off-hours, and creating schedule templates. Increasingly, scheduling is becoming an outsourced service. More about that in section 5. Emerging Areas.

Registration

This streamlines check-in and noting patient's demographic profile information (like name, address, phone, and insurance information). An effective registration function also ensures accurate patient information by managing a Master Patient Index (MPI) with search and retrieval technologies designed to prevent duplicate registrations and errors. Given the right integration with external systems, PM users can determine deductibles, insurance coverage, and collect copay at the time of registering a patient.

Claims Management

This is the doctor's office equivalent to a hospital's Revenue Cycle Management system. It handles the mind-numbingly mundane tasks like creating insurance claims, submitting (and re-submitting) them through clearinghouses, managing denials, remittance tracking, centralized billing, and collection. Most PM systems have some sort of Rules Engine functionality that can be configured for payer nuances and help increase collection and reduce the days a bill remains in accounts receivable.

Analytics

Although the trend toward a comprehensive enterprise-level business intelligence is growing, most Health IT systems continue to provide default reporting and audit functionality. In the same vein, most PM systems allow administrators to query the captured data and create the needed monthly results, financial performance dashboards, and audits reports.

3.6. Personal Health Records

Personal Health Records (PHR) are a befuddling topic to nail down in Health IT because there is a lot of variation in how they are created, sold, and understood. Thankfully, the consistent part of everyone's definition is that the PHR is a set of information that is *accessible to the patient*. In fact, a simple definition would be that a PHR is the patient's view into their own health information. Based on sponsorship, PHRs come in two types: Tethered or Standalone. Both are described below with a deliberate emphasis on extreme ends of feature variations to bring out the contrast.

3.6.1. Tethered PHRs

A tethered PHR is tied to the enterprise EHR of the patient and sponsored by the treating healthcare organization. Being anchored to the formal EHR provides good privacy and security protection for these PHRs. But it also subjects them to the restrictions of the parent organization's policy controls.

A tethered PHR's information is supervised and regulated by the organization that bankrolls it. For example, patients can see their usual lab test results in the tethered PHR, but not sensitive test results (like those for sexual health) because the doctor may choose to withhold that information till after they've had a chance to talk to the patient.

If you exclude e-mail and chat communication features, these type of PHRs are designed for mostly one-way transmission of health information (from the sponsor to patient). That's because getting free-flow, unfiltered information back from the patient is a medico-legal risk for any clinical organization. What if the latest self-reported blood pressure is dangerously high and the patient collapses minutes after submitting it via their PHR? Malpractice claim attorneys would salivate at the possibilities.

Some organizations may employ a "Case Manager" to deal with high-risk patients submitting their health information. That intermediary may reduce the burden and risk on the physician. But typically such workflow would necessitate a dedicated care management software with its own PHR-like module. What we are considering here is a PHR available to all patients of an organization, not just the ones at highest risk.

Tethered PHRs are often so limited in functionality that it seems like a stretch to call them health records at all. If you have corporate health insurance, you most probably have experienced a tethered PHR. They are essentially an online way to see claims history, lab reports, and various forms related to the patient's coverage. Besides that, the bulk content consists of spam-like health education articles and feeble tools like personal risk calculators.

The main drawback of a tethered PHR is the lack of robust access controls and sharing features for patients to use. The web browser's default print and share capabilities don't count in that regard. Additionally, if patients switch providers or insurance, there is no genuinely digital way to take their data with them. The bottom line is that the patient has no real ownership with a tethered PHR.

fragmented paper records, digitizes them, and creates a unified view in an online PHR. Perhaps tackling such "last-mile" of paper records in various doctor's offices is what will make standalone PHRs viable businesses. Without that, all standalone PHRs suffer from a fatal flaw: asking the patient to input their own data.

With health data entry, especially for one's self, it's impractical to expect sustained discipline or accuracy. As human beings, most of us tend to lose interest in things that have no instant or near-term gratification. From this perspective, tethered PHRs may have an advantage because insurers (like Aetna) or providers (like Kaiser Permanente) can automatically populate the PHR with claims-based or archived information like prescriptions, and lab results.

A curious fact about standalone PHRs is that they may fall outside the scope of the HIPAA Privacy Rule. Remember that HIPAA regulations apply to entities that are related to care delivery (like hospitals and insurers). They don't apply if the PHR is offered by an employer (separate from the employer's insurance plan) or made available directly to an individual by a commercial software vendor that is not a HIPAA-covered entity.

Those loopholes don't mean that health software companies can take user privacy any less seriously, of course. But the regulatory burden of HIPAA audits and reporting may be a reason why tethered PHRs' experience feels so encumbered. For example, it's harder to create a nice mobile-friendly version if HIPAA looms over the design, dictating long passwords or short logout times.

3.6.3. The Future of PHRs

So what will this space look like in the next decade? Here are some predictions.

PHRs are and will continue to be necessary. The key to success for tethered PHRs will be data liquidity. When interoperability between various health data silos (like hospitals, insurers, and employers) crosses a critical level, tethered PHRs will gain enviable widespread adoption. Perhaps some sponsors may even let patients take their PHR access with them if they leave. Then patients will self-select into whatever PHR solution that works well for them and use the import/export features to retain it indefinitely.

But that isn't happening for the next 10 years at least. The fundamental incentives of the healthcare market are not changing fast enough to allow data liquidity amongst feuding organizations that soon.

Consumer control over medical records will continue to be a passionate topic, undoubtedly. The romantic notion of standalone PHRs will continue to be funded by venture capital. They will aggregate information from multiple patient portals into one PHR, using evolving standards, regulatory pushes, and better technology like screen scraping. With increasingly smart people focused on the problem, there is a chance we will see a mass-market standalone PHR success story in the next 10 years.

Regardless of being tethered or standalone, any successful PHRs of the future will need to be mobile-friendly and exceptional in their design and usability. Currently, all PHRs seem to splatter unaltered test results and information links in the patient's face without much thought to data presentation and visualization.

Given all that, it wouldn't be surprising if no single company really dominated the market share and got great coverage in terms of connecting to EHR data sources. The PHR market will probably remain fragmented and continue to rely on some amount of manual data entry.

Truth be told, there is a large proportion of the patient population that doesn't care about PHRs. PHR proponents would like to believe these people don't exist, but they do. This subpopulation will continue to feel no need for organizing their records. Hopefully that inaction will fade as the population in general becomes more comfortable with digital records. Patients are really the ultimate viable health information exchange hub. They are the only stakeholder that actively deals in sensitive health information and yet can't commit a HIPAA violation, as their information is their own and they can do whatever they want with it.

3.7. Departmental Systems

Like all large organizations, hospitals are the sum of multiple smaller departments that work together to deliver a spectrum of services to patients. Plenty of Health IT companies got started serving the needs of a niche department's distinct workflow and eventually expanded to cover the healthcare enterprise (e.g. Epic). Most startups today follow the same path because it's easier to find unmet needs and get early customers with a narrowly focused solution.

Nearly all departmental systems may be found bundled with enterprise EHR solutions or as independent best-of-breed systems. We discussed these categories at a high level in section 3.1. Anatomy of an EHR previously.

Integrated departmental systems are part of an overall enterprise suite offered by a single EHR vendor. Theoretically, they have built-in interoperability with other systems and modules of the enterprise EHR. In the real world though, it's not rare to see an integrated departmental system having poor interoperability with the parent EHR. They are rarely purchased and implemented individually, because most are part of a large EHR deployment.

Best-of-breed departmental systems are stand-alones not bundled with a larger EHR. They often service special aspects or subgroups that require more than the generic enterprise system feature set. The following subsections provide short overviews and examples of these key departmental information systems:

- Radiology Systems

- Pathology Information System

- Laboratory Information System

- Emergency Department Information Systems

- Pharmacy Information Systems

- Perioperative Systems

Needless to say, many more departmental systems exist and it's not in the scope of this book to provide details for all. Instead, here is a non-exhaustive list to give you an idea of the diversity out there:

- Obstetrical Information Systems (for Labor & Delivery workflows, Perinatal care)

- Oncology Information Systems

- Surgical Information Systems (Operating Room Information Systems)

- Anesthesia Information Management Systems

- Cardiovascular Information Systems

- Ophthalmology Information Systems

- Rehab Medicine Information Systems

- Respiratory Care Information Systems

- Tissue Tracking Information Systems

3.7.1. Radiology Systems

Radiologists have always lead the pack in terms of adopting information technology, perhaps because their world stopped being analog before any other specialty. The 1970s saw the rise of digital modalities like CT scan and MRI which produced far more images than could be handled through physical films. A CT scan, for example, could yield 20 pages and become unmanageable very fast. It also helped that radiology was a significant revenue generator for most hospitals and executives didn't hesitate to invest in it.

The seeds of digital workflow software were also sown in radiology. As radiology is a mostly volume-based business, the need for scheduling efficiency drove creation of a software category called "Radiology Information Systems" (RIS) in the early 1980s. Many vendors started to offer an RIS to facilitate scheduling, documenting procedures, managing results, and handling billing.

In 1983, the American College of Radiologists (ACR) created a standard called DICOM (Digital Imaging and Communication in Medicine) to enable digital images to be shared independent of proprietary vendor systems. It's commendable that the leaders in radiology had the foresight to work on a standard before things got out of hand in terms of vendor silos. Over the next few years, DICOM became the foundation for transmitting, storing, and printing radiology images across systems. By the early 1990s, a legitimate software category for creating and managing images called "Picture Archiving and Communication System" (PACS) had emerged.

RIS and PACS systems have since transformed how radiology is practiced. Radiologists graduating their residency program today are unfamiliar with paper films and can actually practice from anywhere (a less-talked-about aspect of the telemedicine transformation).

Consider that an average 16-slice CT scan produces a file around 250Mb in size and that an estimated 600 million imaging procedures are done annually in the U.S. This means that medical imaging data in U.S. will cross the 1 exabyte mark in 2016. An exabyte is a million terabytes, in case you didn't know. Radiology is undoubtedly the first clinical field which has seen a complete paradigm shift solely due to health information technology advances.

Here is a quick feature overview of the two systems:

RIS

- Patient registration, appointment scheduling, coordination of the needed imaging location and resources to ensure that nothing conflicts and the patient visit is successful.

- Tracking radiology procedure phases like: physician's order, insurance authorization, patient visit, imaging done, images available, radiologist reviewed and reported, report transcribed, and critical results notified back to ordering physician. Consistent process milestones and automated tracking numbers for each image enables detailed operational reporting and benchmarking. Tracking metrics in this manner improves radiology practice efficiency and quality.

- Documentation like consent forms, contrast allergy records, contrast medication records, and interventional radiology procedure notes.

- Interpretation management tools like radiologist work lists (also called task lists) which outline the available unread studies based on factors such as patient status, care setting, referring physician, and location.

- Results distribution back to the ordering physician's EHR, and in some cases, to patient portals or PHRs.

- Billing and reimbursement management.

PACS

- The hardware display of a PACS system needs to be of certain high-resolution and pixel depth so that it can accommodate different imaging modalities consistently.

- Image manipulation features allow radiologists to easily manage and view images. These include customizable protocol shortcuts, quick-access navigation menus, and image tools like rotate/pan/zoom/roll/tilt.

- Workflow management tools allow users to organize their radiology work in certain ways (like by body areas, care settings, or modality) and report out using templates and pre-populated fields. Speech recognition has been widely used in these workflows since early 2000s, which is perhaps another first-to-adopt distinction for radiology.

- System performance and architecture is a critical attribute for PACS, given the exabyte-scale of image data being stored, retrieved, archived, queried. These systems have benefitted from the storage, processing, and graphics technology advances elsewhere (notably the computer gaming industry).

- Besides radiology, other clinical areas like cardiology, oncology, and gastroenterology can leverage the PACS infrastructure to incorporated their imaging needs.

Today, a radiologist's workflow originates when an imaging order is created within hospital- and office-based EHR systems. It ends when the images and radiologist's report are available within the originating EHR systems. The return on investment (ROI) for Health IT in radiology comes not only from eliminating film production and storage costs, but also via improving productivity by enabling remote consultations, faster turnarounds, and more accurate diagnoses. No other field can boast radical shifts of this scale achieved through progress in information technology.

3.7.2. Digital Pathology

Pathology is a unique clinical field that exclusively deals with diagnosis of disease. Just like radiology, the information technology revolution seeds were planted in pathology when the tools started becoming digital. In the 1990s digital microscopes became a reality and the analog image of a pathology slide was converted to pixels stored and manipulated by computers.

Like radiology, the digital imaging process in pathology includes four key steps:

1. Image capture
2. Image manipulation and annotation
3. Image storage and management
4. Image display and sharing

The key technology advancement to note here is "Whole Slide Imaging" (WSI, also referred to as virtual or wide-field microscopy) which involves digitization of glass slides to produce high-resolution digital images at multiple magnifications and focal planes. WSI has been hobbled by the lack of a clear standard like DICOM, but efforts are underway. Currently digital slides in pathology are generally well accepted, especially in education, where annotation, sharing and archiving are important.

Even though the field has lagged behind radiology, no one doubts that digital pathology is the future. But it's debatable when that future will arrive. Pathology organizations and vendors have continuously evangelized the digitization cause for the last two decades but a significant resistance to change remains in the clinical ranks.

When the tipping point arrives, expect even more data management and storage challenges as colored images are bulkier than black-and-white radiographs. Dermatology, another image-oriented field, would be a logical next frontier for a color-image workflow system.

3.7.3. Laboratory Information Systems

The software supporting a modern laboratory's operations is known as a Laboratory Information System (LIS). Although one can certainly find evidence for rudimentary attempts at LIS as far back as the early 1960s, none of the early forays proved successful at execution or adoption till mid-1980s when commercial vendors started emerging.

There are lots of variations in this segment of healthcare. Besides the variations in test inventory, labs can be private or small, independent or part of a regional network, owned by a vendor or hospital system. They can serve physicians, hospitals, employers, insurers, or cater directly to patients.

Integrated LISs provide laboratory workflows within a larger EHR and are offered as a part of the overall enterprise suite offered by the EHR vendor. *Best-of-breed* LISs are stand-alone systems that usually service a special aspect or domain. For example: anatomic pathology, microbiology, transfusion medicine (blood bank), transplant medicine, and molecular and genetic diagnostics are all sub-domains with unique requirements that are not usually satisfied by the features and content of a generic enterprise system.

Here are the major features found in a typical LIS:

push to declare the existence of a cousin to LIS: the Laboratory Information Management System (LIMS). LIMS is used in research and manufacturing facilities for industries like pharmaceuticals and chemicals. Its industrial design is meant for dealing with large batches of samples, and demanding scientists as users. In cases where clinical care and research co-exist, LIMS and LIS may be less distinguishable.

3.7.4. Emergency Department Information Systems

There is no denying that the Emergency Department (ED) is on the short list of money-making departments of a health system. Unscheduled visits are risky, costly, and short, so digitization is a natural boon to ED work. Anticipated benefits from an ED Information System (EDIS) includes improved throughput, reduced costs, better compliance, and increased revenues.

Feature-wise, what sets an EDIS apart from other generic systems is the fact that it's not designed for longitudinal care. It's about optimizing and coordinating a short patient encounter in a very litigious environment. Typical features include:

- *Registration*: Uniquely identifying every incoming ED patient has its own challenges. Most patients can provide the information needed by the front desk registration staff, but it's not uncommon to get an unconscious and unaccompanied person who provides identification only after their record has been created and partially populated. Such "John Doe" registration workflows of creating, merging, and linking patient records are key for EDIS.

- *Documentation*: This helps ED nurses, physicians, and other staff complete documentation like triage forms, History & Physical, discharges instructions, and admission note. Given the fast pace of ED work, documentation speed is a key metric (i.e. with the minimum number of clicks).

- *Patient Tracking*: This follows the patient's physical location and care throughout ED, and displays information like patient's location, assigned staff, and completed or pending tasks. It's a centralized view to replace the iconic whiteboard-based coordination.

- *Operations*: It's easy for EDIS to create an overall picture of ED bed utilization and availability because it tracks each patient's whereabouts. It can even automate equipment tracking for items like infusion pumps, monitors, and gurneys. All that operational flow information is useful for calibrating staffing levels.

- *Administration*: As with all departmental systems, tracking key performance metrics and reporting on them is an essential part of EDIS. Metrics like patient volume, average wait time, and number of admissions are typically prioritized.

- *Charge Capture*: Charging for services provided depends on how well events have been documented. Besides the obvious financial consequences, efficient billing also affects ED physician contracts and a department's ability to maintain qualified physicians.

- *Staffing*: EDs operate 24 hours a day, 7 days a week. Coordinating aspects like staff levels, vacations, backups, and projections are very important functions.

- *Compliance*: Satisfying regulatory requirements from organizations like JointCommission.org and EMTALA, capturing data for regional and/or national databases, and reporting to key surveillance programs are additional requirements.[24] Other standard features include order entry, results reporting, integrations with other internal and external systems.

ED Market

Simply put, ED is one of the top-grossing parts of a hospital and its profile is growing in importance. It's generally accepted that the average non-trauma ED generates 20% of a hospital's profits by triggering admissions. ED visit rates increased by more than a third between 1997 and 2007.[25] That trend will only increase as the Affordable Care Act creates more insured potential patients.[26] New formats like Free-Standing EDs (FSEDs) located in or near shopping centers are targeting consumers with private insurance. FSEDs are growing fast too. In 2009, there were 241 such facilities, 65% more than the 146 counted just five years prior. By 2013 the number had doubled again to more than 400.[27]

There are many examples of young companies trying to reinvent the ED experience. iTriageHealth.com (acquired by Aetna in 2012) was one of the first to provide real-time "ED wait times" functionality with which a patient could avoid packed facilities. Nashville, TN based InQuicker.com allows patients to hold their spot online in the urgent care or ER waiting room queues.

Another company called MyHealthDirect.com provides a subscription-based system for facilitating the exchange of scheduling information in a community, so that overburdened ERs can triage away non-emergent cases with a confirmed outpatient clinic appointment. The alternative would be for the ER staff or case worker to call other clinics and manually confirm appointments—a predictably slow and inefficient process.

3.7.5. Pharmacy Information Systems

The science and workflow of pharmacy revolves around drugs. The features of a Pharmacy Information System (PIS) are easier to describe in relation to the lifecycle of medications: from when they are procured to after they are given to the patient.

Inventory and Purchasing

Most pharmacies stock more than a thousand items and require the continuous work of purchasing management. Monitoring drug utilization, placing orders with drug manufacturers and distributors, and eventually receiving, invoicing, tracking, and refilling prescriptions are key functions for a PIS. All of these steps become even more sensitive in case of highly scrutinized substances like narcotics.

Prescription Review

The wheels of the clinical workflow are set in motion when a physician prescribes medications using CPOE. A fully-featured PIS would enable a pharmacist to review these prescriptions for safety and efficacy. That review would require patient-specific information like allergies, lab results, indications, dose and routes of medication, prescription instructions, and clinical objectives.

Comprehensive drug knowledge bases are also needed as a reference for content like drug-drug interactions, side effects, and drug recalls. Today, four major commercial vendors dominate the market space for these kind of knowledge bases: First DataBank (fdbhealth.com), Wolters Kluwer Health (wolterskluwercdi.com), Cerner Multum (multum.com), and Thomson Micromedex (micromedex.com). Additionally, the federally-funded National Library of Medicine offers a free alternative called RxNorm (nlm.nih.gov/research/umls/rxnorm).

4.1. Anatomy of an HIE

Section 2. Landscape discussed how HIEs came about and why we need them. To summarize, HIEs are focused on facilitating information exchange *between* participating care organizations (and not *inside* an organization, like EHRs). The information exchange can be thought of in two ways: a data push or a data pull.

The "Push" model is a send-first approach. Once the originator (sender) knows that it has something to publish, it sends the data out without any request from a destination (receiver). Common SMS text messages are a good example of this. The "Pull" model, on the other hand, makes the sender wait passively till an information request from the receiver comes in. That's what happens in RSS feeds, for example.

In the world of health information exchange, these same models respectively translate to "Directed" and "Query-based."

Directed Exchange

In 2010, ONC championed an initiative called "Direct Project" (directproject.org) which specified the technical standards and services necessary for creating push-based interoperability. Simply put, Direct's version of interoperability behaves like e-mail with fortified security features.

Besides dictating the underlying transport protocol, Direct Project created a new, distinct business/technical entity called a "Health Information Service Provider" (HISP). A HISP is responsible for services like digital certificates and trust management that are needed for directed exchange. To draw a rough parallel from the consumer-internet e-mail space, direct protocol is like SMTP and HISPs are like e-mail provider services (e.g. Gmail and Yahoo!Mail).

Consumer e-mail services revolutionized individual communication decades ago. Today anyone can get an e-mail address for free and send a message to anyone else who has one, regardless of which service provider they have. Directed exchange has similar potential for liberating common back-and-forth communication in healthcare. It can make faxes extinct and phone calls rare. Simple workflows like referrals and prescription refills can easily be done through this push-based architecture.

We will discuss Directed Exchange and its fate a bit more in section 4.5. Service Layer.

Query-based Exchange

This is where systems and interfaces are set up to perform on-demand discovery of patient information in the records aggregated by the HIE. For example, consider the case of a patient who suffers a medical emergency during vacationing away from home. Providers performing that unplanned care can still look up the patient's vital medication or allergy information, even though the records are not local. Their systems simply request that information from the patient's main provider through the query-based HIE.

Great as that system is, it's also more complex and expensive than Directed Exchange. All the devilish details of finding the correct patient records; ensuring security, privacy, and consent; storing, transmitting, and standardizing care records etc. need to be figured out before queries are viable and responses useful.

Patient's role

The official federal view on push/pull exchange includes a third form of exchange, called the "Consumer-mediated Exchange."[29] It is based on the premise that patients can be their own pivot for information exchange. Just like individuals manage their financial information through online banking; patients with access to their medical records could manage the exchange of health information.

It's hard to see the point of this third category. The other two are distinct technical architecture approaches, whereas consumer-mediated exchange seems to be an attempt to remain politically correct. The theoretical channels for consumers to be the exchange hub are many: They can verbally transmit takeaways from a previous doctor to a new one, or endure the painful process of getting paper copies of medical records, or use an online PHR as the tool. If the argument here is in favor of classifying online PHRs or portals as another type of HIE, it's a confounding one because even those tools use either a push or pull architecture.

4.1.1. HIE the Noun

Some background context for understanding the HIE market was already explored in section 4. Health Information Exchanges. Let's cover a few ways to categorize the entity we call an HIE. First and most importantly, they can be classified according to funding source.

Public HIEs

These are paid for by taxpayer money, most of which was distributed by the HITECH Act in 2009 to create regional and state-level HIEs. Today that wellspring has nearly dried up and self-sustainability has become the main problem for public HIEs. Concerns about cooperating with competition and data ownership have consistently made stakeholders unwilling to pay for public HIE services. There is a somewhat dated dashboard on the HealthIT.gov website that provides high-level details on public HIE efforts.[30]

There has also been lots of press given to a national-level HIE effort called the "Nationwide Health Information Network" (or NwHIN). Here is what you need to know about NwHIN: It's not an actual network or HIE but rather a set of policies. Even the HealthIT.gov website defines it as "a set of standards, services, and policies that enable secure health information exchange over the Internet."[31]

Private HIEs

These are sponsored by a commercial entity (usually a hospital system) to help direct business from peripheral clinics and affiliated providers to themselves. The argument for private HIEs being the future of the HIE market has previously been laid out in section 2.3. Health Information Exchanges. Organizations looking to create tight clinical networks to better coordinate care and keep costs low will need to create private HIEs. As Obamacare changes the payment models, private HIEs will increasingly serve as the operating system for the surviving large hospitals and IDNs.

Another useful way to classify HIEs is according to their data storage architecture.

Centralized

In this architectural approach, all HIE participants send the previously-agreed-upon data to a common central store (called the "Clinical Data Repository", or CDR) which is created and maintained by the HIE. This approach yields better performance (i.e. faster query-response times), but is expensive because extensive infrastructure investment and data agreements are needed upfront.

More importantly, the centralized model requires strong coordination and political alignment to truly succeed. Which is why this architecture is almost always seen in case of private HIEs owned by a single entity with complete operational authority.

Federated

Also known as the "Decentralized" or "Distributed" model, it has no single central CDR. Instead, HIE data is stored in a collection of repositories that participating organizations own and maintain locally. In a strictly federated model every request for patient data is passed along to every participating data source. As you can imagine, that only works as long as the volume of requests and the number of nodes being pinged remains low.

Having patient records across multiple remote locations means duplication and constant confusion about which information is most up-to-date. To its credit, the federated approach doesn't have a single point of failure and is politically more feasible because participating independent (and often competing) organizations can retain physical control of data physically (a pointless concern that plagues many healthcare executives).

Hybrid

This approach uses a centralized virtual index of which patient's data is stored where, using an indexing service called RLS (Record Locator Service). In effect, this takes the best of both centralized and federated approaches to store some data centrally while using an RLS to get to the rest. As the geographical reach of an HIE gets larger, a hybrid approach becomes inevitable.

4.1.2. Functional Layers of an HIE

Below is a high-level list of what an ideal HIE should do. Each translates to a conceptual layer in the HIE architecture and is detailed in the sections that follow.

1. An HIE needs to accept incoming data, validate it, normalize it, and then store or pass it along to destination. The mechanics of all that are in the "Data Layer."

2. Systems that receive HIE data have their own context and specifications for consuming that information. The HIE functionality that deals with that repackaging is in the "Transformation Layer."

3. The ability to present HIE data to end users comes from the "Presentation Layer." This is what produces the Longitudinal Patient Record (LPR) I described previously.

4. An ideal HIE follows service-oriented architecture (SOA) principles to create a "Services Layer" that enables conversations between numerous IT systems and creates functionality that can be reused across networks.

5. It's logical for an HIE to generate reports and insights on the troves of data it holds and processes. Those features are enabled in the "Analytics Layer."

Note that this layered-view framework doesn't leave a clean room for placing usual large IT system features like backup and recovery, and user management. Hence those are omitted intentionally. Also, the caveat from section 3.1.1 on the volatility of EHRs applies here as well: It is futile to claim a complete feature list because the functional definition of an HIE keeps evolving as vendors do their best to adapt to changing market needs.

4.2. Data Layer

HIEs are made up of multiple partner organizations that own disparate, scattered versions of a patient's data. Therefore, if there is one central functionality that all HIEs are expected to have, it is managing the variations of data from originating systems. Architecturally speaking, this means doing three things: Aggregation, Normalization, and Orchestration.

4.2.1. Architectural View of Data Layer

Aggregation

Data flows across health organizations as formatted messages in a feed stream. For example, a patient discharge message will be in a format called "ADT," lab results in "ORU," orders in "ORM," and financial charges in "DFT."

Consider that an average hospital gets tens of thousands of patient visits a year and has multiple IT applications generating messages for every significant event. It's easy to reach a message volume in the double-digit millions. Now multiply that by the number of participating organizations in a given HIE. The end scenario is an always-active set of machines spewing dissimilar digital data, creating a frenzy of back-and-forth message exchange.

Assembling all that chaos into a common dataset is the goal of aggregation. It's a critical task because incoming data needs to be managed in a consistent fashion. For example, policies like security and retention should be applied systematically. Sometimes, aggregation may include some straightforward cleaning of the received data to fix common issues of syntactical conformance, like extra trailing characters, or out-of-order HL7 segments.

Normalization

Normalization takes the aggregated data one step further by reducing it to unique, valid attributes. Incoming data for normalization can be different in terms of syntax (its grammatical structure) or semantics (what it means).

Typical syntactic variations result from the diversity of industry-accepted message formats like HL7 v2, HL7 v3, HIPAA EDI, CCDs, and FHIR. Semantic variations, on the other hand, come from multiple controlled terminologies like ICD, SNOMED, LOINC, and CPT.

Here are some examples of normalization issues:

- One system sends "Benazepril 10mg" as NDC code 54868235002 and another system sends "Captopril 25mg" as RxNorm code 197436. Both drugs belong to the category of "ACE inhibitors" and the resulting record needs to show a cumulative list for that category of drugs. So the HIE would need to merge those two records based on the meaning (semantics) of the contained data points.

- Converting the simple pipe-delimited message format of HL7 v2.x used by an originating system to the markup-heavy, XML-based HL7 v3.x used by destination system.

- The same Hemoglobin A1c test being referred to as "HbA1c" in one feed, "A1c" in another, and "Glycosylated Hemoglobin" in the rest.

There are many more transformations that can be applied to messages. At times the incoming message has data about one aspect, but missing or outdated information on another, such as expired insurance information, a missing transaction number, or wrong patient address. In these cases, the HIE can enhance the original message and make it more accurate before passing along to the intended recipient.

Messages also need to be evaluated for completeness and checked for all required fields being populated. Most messages end up being only about 90% compliant with established standards because custom fields, characters, or codes creep in. Blame non-compliance on immature systems, unkempt interfaces, or an abject lack of standards for that specific information, but it happens.

Think of normalization as the process where a known template is used to recognize attributes of interest and remove anything that is duplicate or unknown. Good design practice would dictate that the HIE still retains the original message data in archive, because the definition of what is normal may change over time. If nothing else, keeping full records is almost always aligned with some kind of legal requirement.

Advances in indexing and searching unstructured data will continue to decrease the normalization overhead, so hopefully the importance of this capability will fade in future.

Orchestration

Ultimately, all the data coming into an HIE is ticketed for a prearranged destination. For example, a referral from a patient's PCP is addressed to a specialist in the HIE network. So the concluding task of the HIE data layer would be to manage the routing of the normalized messages and attached documents to the intended recipient.

4.2.2. Modular View of Data Layer

These architectural descriptions will most certainly elicit different interpretations and opinions from experts. For example, some may argue that normalization is really just transformation, or that enhancing an incomplete message is part of aggregation. There is no right answer. It all depends on the preference and design direction of those who create the HIE blueprint. But irrespective of architecture, certain functional modules remain vital to dealing with HIE data. Here are the main ones:

Master Patient Index

Each participating organization in an HIE invariably has its own Medical Record Number (MRN) or a similar identifier for a given patient. With multiple organizations submitting information about one patient, ensuring that the person in question is correctly identified at every source becomes a complex task. If HIE is the body, Master Patient Index (MPI) is its backbone, dedicated to the task of holding all the information together.

There are two basic approaches for creating record-matching algorithms in an MPI: deterministic and probabilistic. Deterministic matching does field-by-field comparison to find exact matches and has no tolerance for errors. It rejects commonly occurring discrepancies like loose nicknames, old home addresses, and married vs. maiden last name. As you might expect, this approach results in more false-negative matches and duplicated records.

A probabilistic MPI uses flexible logic to deal with the nuances of identification information. Weighted scores are given for different data aspects to create a likelihood score that the information belongs to a specific known person. A probabilistic approach can better deal with variations like phonetic spellings, regional variations, and incomplete or erroneous data. These match results tend to have more false positives and frequently require manual confirmations.

Even with sophisticated algorithms sifting through the details, it would be audacious to say that MPI is a fully-automated part of the HIE. A lot of MPI functionality remains dedicated to the registration staff's supervisory workflows around creating, evaluating, and resolving queues of unmatched identities and other errors.

There is an ongoing debate about adopting a universal patient identifier that can be standardized across the nation. The preexisting financial ties of Social Security Numbers (SSNs) makes them a very risky single-point-of-failure in case of breaches. Proponents say that combining just the last four digits of a person's SSN with other demographic information can make identification many times more accurate.

Most HIE vendors create their own basic patient matching, and partner for advanced functionality with vendors in the Master Data Management (MDM) space.

Record Locator Service

The Record Locator Service (RLS) serves as a catalog of references to the patient-specific information located across an HIE network. Note that the RLS only stores pointers to where patient information lies, and not the actual information itself. Synergistically working with MPI which pinpoints a patient, an RLS identifies where the records reside for that unique patient. Using MPI and RLS in conjunction, an HIE can stitch together comprehensive virtual patient records on demand from the submitting source systems.

Clinical Data Repository

A Clinical Data Repository (CDR) is the core database that combines and stores patient data submitted by multiple sources. In their least effective form, CDRs are simple databases that securely hold data and don't do much else. The more advanced CDRs are sophisticated data warehouses with models that intelligently map contained data with organizational needs. They can adapt to new data definitions and schema changes and are optimized for analytics and research.

All HIE member organizations have their own CDR, of course. But in centralized HIEs, there exists a central CDR that hosts a common denominator of information and is accessible by all organizations.

Interface Engine

Interface engines are where the rubber hits the road in terms of mapping incompatible data sources of an HIE. They are software conduits that use standard protocols and transactions sets to connect various communication end-points.

Based on configurable rules, the management tools of an interface engine can perform actions like routing transactions, processing formats, converting protocols, extracting data, sending notifications, providing status dashboards, and report on errors.

Most HIE vendors use a third-party offering as their interface engine. Some big names in this space are: CorepointHealth.com, Ensemble by InterSystems.com, Rhapsody by OrionHealth.com, Cloverleaf by Infor.com, and Express Connect by Summit-Healthcare.com.

4.3. Transformation Layer

HIEs exist to reduce the need for one-to-one connections between multiple systems. The Data Layer ingests feeds from originating systems and processes it with logic that is common and indisputable. However, destination systems may have their own specifications on what data they accept, when, and how. These context-specific sets of manipulations are managed by the Transformation Layer of an HIE. Some key examples of transformation are given below with the common suffix of "Gateway."

4.3.1. Public Health Gateway

The hierarchy of governmental public health systems in the United States is comprised of federal agencies, state health agencies, tribal and territorial health departments, and local health departments. Every state formally monitors certain health conditions based on its population and environment. For example, New York monitors nine different syndromic categories: Respiratory, GI, Fever, Asthma, Neurological, Rash, Carbon Monoxide, Heat Wave, and Hypothermia. California collects infectious diseases lab reports, cancer cases, and blood lead test results.

Patient-level information submitted from counties and regions provides the individual counts, as well as short-and-long term trend graphs to administrative officials. All that data comes from the information systems of healthcare organizations treating those patients. Collecting that information of interest, normalizing it in the required format (dictated by the state health authority), and submitting is one of the primary use cases for an HIE. And it's executed by the Public Health Gateway.

This "Syndromic Surveillance" value proposition is not just about one-way submission from provider organizations to state agencies. It also facilitates bi-directional communication. State departments of health need queries to run on a specified or ad-hoc schedule so that they can monitor the data from the HIE without requiring any submission from providers. For policymakers, these custom data feed subscriptions represent a crucial pulse on community and statewide health status.

4.3.2. Immunization Gateway

Every U.S. state and territory has chosen to track immunizations given to individuals within their geopolitical area, especially children under 6 years. Today 59 "Immunization Registries" (also called Immunization Information Systems, or IISs) are supported by government grants and managed by public health departments. In some cases, healthcare provider participation is mandated by state law; in others it's voluntary.[32]

Immunization registries allow clinicians to query the IIS database and determine the history of vaccination for a given patient. If they subsequently administer a vaccine, that new record needs to be submitted to the registry. At a population level these registries provide valuable aggregate insights for guiding state policies and health initiatives.

An Immunization Gateway facilitates the exchange between an HIE and state immunization registries. Usually that means both enabling the clinician to query the registry for immunization history of a given patient, and also creating batches of files from the immunization data generated by HIE member organizations and sending them at configurable intervals to the respective state registry.

Immunizations are a part of the public health dataset, so it can be argued that they logically belong to the Public Health Gateway's scope of work. However, they deserve to be a separate category based on their importance.

4.3.3. Personal Health Record (PHR) Gateway

As explained previously in section 3. Electronic Health Records, PHRs allow patients to view and manage their own health information. The PHR Gateway is what facilitates bi-directional exchange between an HIE and the chosen PHR(s). The usual data types exchanged are medications, immunizations, allergies, problems (diagnoses), lab results and radiology reports.

The obvious use of a PHR Gateway is for organizations like hospitals, clinics, and labs to send information to the patient. The reverse is also true, though. Using a PHR Gateway's capabilities, patients are enabled to share their existing PHR data with other providers in the HIE.

But a PHR Gateway is not merely a dumb pipe that is carrying information back and forth. Below are some examples of the nuances it needs to deal with, clearly justifying its existence as an independent HIE product.

- *Information blocking*: Updates from an originating system can't be allowed to pass without inspection. For example, lab results or diagnoses around sensitive topics like HIV or STDs need to be held back till the physician has had a chance to talk to the patient. This would require a user interface where providers (or system administrators on their behalf) can place restrictions on what information needs to be blocked and for how long. The rules for such restrictions can be applied at different levels: for a practice, for a location, for all patients of a specific provider, or even for a specific patient. Under the covers it also means figuring out which providers are currently authorized to access a patient's information and alerting them about new updates on that patient.

- *Information filtering*. The trends of care management have given rise to condition-specific PHRs that focus on a category like mental health or pregnancy. For connecting with such niche information destinations, a PHR Gateway needs to filter patient data based on the conditions of interest for that destination system.

- *Subscription management*: A patient may decide, at any time, to subscribe or unsubscribe from getting information in or sending information out of their PHR. Managing access control is also important. Third-party systems like EHR that create clinical data need to be white-listed and authorized to deposit information in a PHR.

The PHR Gateway provides a cautionary reminder that technological capability doesn't always mean technological adoption. Getting information into a patient's PHR is all fine, but the reverse flow is not exactly a feature cherished by all providers. It's not hard to understand why: EHR is a medico-legal record. The EHR-sponsoring provider organization is assuming the responsibility of being aware of everything within that formal document. There are severe legal consequences if any critical information in an EHR is not acted upon.

For example, consider the case of a patient who takes blood pressure readings after a morning run. If the patient collapses a few days later because of a pre-existing ailment, those high blood pressure readings are surely going to surface in a malpractice lawsuit, suggesting the care provider ignored abnormal data in the EHR. That's a hyperbolic example, of course, but one can imagine many other situations where the continuous inflow of patient-generated data creates a need for constant monitoring at the provider's end.

The takeaway here is that technology advances need to be accompanied by process changes. For example, case managers could be staffed and trained to review patient-generated data. In fact, a PHR Gateway can be a key tool for the care management of patients with chronic conditions. Combined with sensor-based devices (like activity bands, weighing scales, and glucometers), it can create the remote monitoring infrastructure that enables patients to stay at home and avoid emergencies.

The trend around health consumers who actively participate in their medical care has been dubbed the "ePatient" movement. Depending on who you ask, the "e-" prefix stands for empowered, enabled, equipped, or engaged. It's a fantastic positive shift in the healthcare market, undoubtedly. But the euphoria behind it shouldn't smother the legal and procedural constraints of a real-world execution. The PHR Gateway is a good example of a technology frontier that can help in solving those constraints.

4.3.4. Image Gateway

As a data type, images are distinct enough to require their own workflows and tools in EHRs (see section 3.7.1. Radiology Systems). The same holds true in HIEs. An Image Gateway provides access to diagnostic-quality medical images by connecting the HIE to an underlying "Image Exchange."

Image Exchanges are a relatively new artifact in the Health IT market. For a long time, the majority of the data being exchanged though HIEs was text-based (like patient demographics, medications, allergies, diagnoses and problems). Explicit media discussions about Image Exchanges started around 2009 with a marketing push from companies like eHealthTechnologies.com and lifeIMAGE.com that were promoting their own software products. These exchanges were proposed to complement the text-heavy HIEs by allowing care teams to quickly access medical images from the whole network regardless of where they were originally captured. They did so by connecting to and centralizing the imaging data from various local PACS systems, EHRs, and other data repositories.

The benefits have been obvious: more timely treatment, fewer duplicate procedures, and better coverage in remote areas. Besides vendors who make the software (i.e. the capability), there are also explicit image-sharing networks (i.e. the community). For example: "Image Share" by the behemoth industry organization RSNA.org, and "PowerShare Network" by software giant Nuance.com.

Here are some of the major capabilities of an Image Exchange:

- *Viewing an image*: Launching a radiology image through a web-based viewing platform.

- *Community-wide work list*: To collect, sort, assign, and view the various imaging studies.

- *Collaboration*: Tools to consult with other care providers in the community for second opinions and referrals.

- *Integration*: Local interfaces that enable users to access images directly from within their institutional EHRs and/or PACS.

4.3.5. Order Gateway

According to the American Clinical Laboratory Association (acla.com), more than 7 billion tests are performed in the U.S. each year by around 322,000 clinical labs, 80% of which are classified as small businesses. Every year, billions of lab orders generated by physicians are sent to this fragmented lab market and every one of those orders tries to make its way back to the sender as a result report.

Within an HIE ecosystem, the Order Gateway enables this bidirectional transport between ordering providers and testing labs. It makes the end-to-end process traceable as routing happens between multiple parties. It tracks the order lifecycle through various states like in-process, partially resulted, final result, cancelled, changed, and completed.

Transporting results back from order-fulfilling lab systems (like LIS) to the order-placing provider systems (like EHR) requires functionality like:

- *Association*: Matching a lab result to the order that initiated the testing

- *Identification*: Pinpointing the right patient and ordering physician. For example, replacing the patient identifier from the laboratory with the one that EHR uses, or vice versa.

- *Message processing*: Beyond acting as just a transport layer, this Gateway can transform and validate messages flowing through. It provides workflow tools like message search and editing, feed configuration, and error management.

4.3.6. EDI Gateway

When the Health Insurance Portability and Accountability Act (HIPAA) was passed in 1996, it required that health insurers comply with the health-specific electronic data interchange (EDI) standards established by the government. EDI is the arrangement that allows automated trading and processing of information by computers, without human intervention. National standards for EDI have been developed for many industries (not just healthcare) to avoid the expense and complexity of dealing with multiple proprietary formats.

There are many HIPAA-mandated EDI standard transactions and code sets in use today.[33] For example, transaction "270" is used by a provider to request eligibility, coverage, co-pay, and other benefit information from a payer. Payers then to respond such a request by using a "271" transaction. Similarly, a health claim status request is submitted via 276 transaction and response is sent back as a 277.

Besides Medicare and Medicaid, there are more than 800 commercial insurers in the market that actively perform health information transactions. And that number doesn't account for the multiple "Clearinghouses" that act as a conduit between claim submitters and claim payers. All of these organizations have variations in the exchange and communication protocols. The real-life process of connecting them ends up being a maze of

VPN connections, FTP/SFTP, web services, and phone calls. That's where an EDI Gateway can add value.

It creates one simple connection to payer networks for all the participating organizations in the HIE. The insurance eligibility functionality can be integrated into front-desk staff's workflow such that it can be done for individual patients or in batch for upcoming patient appointments.

4.3.7. ePrescribing Gateway

We have discussed ePrescribing (eRx) previously in section 3.4. Computerized Provider Order Entry. It's an indisputable trend buoyed by reform regulations. A monopoly on a nationwide eRx network lies with a private company called Surescripts.

Instead of each health system, hospital, or clinic making its own connection with Surescripts, the HIE offers a way to centralize through the ePrescribing Gateway. With it, a physician in the HIE can review a patient's plan eligibility, prescription history, approved formularies, etc. instantly at the time of prescribing. The resulting prescription can then be routed on the Surescripts network and delivered to the patient's choice of pharmacy.

Admittedly, it's a bit generous to give eRx a "Gateway" in this case. Most other gateways discussed here enable bidirectional communication between two sets of multiple information systems. But in eRx's case, the relation is so solitarily focused on one company that it may be justifiable to call this the "Surescripts Connector."

4.4. Presentation Layer

The Presentation Layer is where an HIE becomes tangible for the end user, offering a unified display of information called the Longitudinal Patient Record (LPR). We started talking about the LPR in section 2. The Landscape, highlighting how it's different from an EHR. Although LPR is the term of choice for this book, there are synonyms out there: Community Health Record, Patient-Centric Record, HIE Patient Record, Consolidated Patient Record, Composite Health Record, to name a few.

The classic use case scenario for an LPR goes like this: a patient comes in for the first time to see a provider that participates in a regional HIE. Using a web-based LPR viewer, the provider pulls up existing clinical information (like current medications, allergies, and health problems) from all across the HIE network. That insight prevents duplicate tests and prescription errors, and produces better outcomes at reduced costs. Everyone lives happily ever after.

4.4.1. Functionality That Doesn't Belong Here

That ideal scenario also points to the Achilles' heel of the Presentation Layer: over-expectation. As it gets used for care delivery, the utility hopes from LPR invariably go beyond what we want from a network-wide clinical information viewer. Users start expecting an all-encompassing clinical workflow tool that has all the needed functionality. A stellar example of this happens when HIEs offer EHR-like functionality.

To understand that, let's go back to the early days of the HIE market when some of the organizations joining a local HIE were still paper-based offices that had not moved to EHRs. For them, the HIE membership was a quick way to get on the electronic records bandwagon, a small step toward modernization that didn't require much workflow or organization change. On the flip side, the local HIE leadership was happy to dangle an "EHR-lite" module as an incentive to increase membership and get regional coverage.

That's how the regrettable trend of putting EHR features like CPOE and Documentation into HIEs started. Choosing to deliver a highly-localized workflow (like CPOE) in a context that crosses organizational boundaries (like HIE) is a setup for eventual failure. Even if one can smoothen out local variations and create a one-size-fits-all workflow suitable for an HIE, there is a difference in evolutionary impact of regulations. For example, Meaningful Use regulations are driving EHRs toward functionality like ePrescribing and drug interaction checks. None of those are central to the mission of an HIE software.

The point here is not about advocating a holy separation between EHRs and HIEs. Instead, it's about maintaining focus. There are significant opportunity costs in offering EHR-like features and HIE vendors have succumbed time and again to the temptation of duplicating EHR use cases. That should explain the confusing, crisscross marketing of the big name Health IT companies (like Optum.com and McKesson.com) as well as the aspiring ones (like Edifecs.com). The ideal situation would be for EHRs and HIEs to provide complementary and interoperable offerings.

4.4.2. Functionality That Belongs

Messaging

Faxes, phone calls, and paper letters are the way providers usually communicate beyond their organization's boundary. Insecure e-mails or texts are a liability risk, thanks to HIPAA. But a common electronic messaging capability within an HIE network could allow providers to exchange updates and clinical content with each other. Besides the cost savings from reducing fax and phone-tag, there is the obvious advantage of improving care coordination and outcomes. "Messaging" in an HIE can range from simple text-like push messages to complex workflows that happen on top of messages.

In its simplest form, HIE messaging feels like the familiar e-mail inbox. Under the hood though, it has added security features like at-rest and in-transit encryption, verified sender/receivers, etc. The boon in this area was the initiation of a transport standard called "Direct" (discussed more in section 4.1. Anatomy of an HIE and section 4.5. Services Layer).

The complex-workflow end of messaging is best exemplified by the electronic "Referral Management" use case. In fact, facilitating referrals electronically is one of the main selling points of an HIE. It's worthwhile to examine this separately.

Referral Management

The referral process begins when a physician determines if they need to direct their patient to another provider for care. Usually a referral goes from a PCP to a specialist, although specialist-to-specialist referrals also happen. Referrals are not simple redirects. Besides figuring out whom to refer the patient to, the referring physician needs to ensure that there is a clinically warranted reason, which service(s) to authorize, and for how long.

Most referral arrangements are based on mutually-agreed guidelines between the referring and referred-to parties. These guidelines are literature-driven protocols for common diagnoses that describe the test, therapies, or treatments a provider should perform before referring. These guidelines are usually supplied by the medical groups themselves (sometimes in cooperation with their specialists) or bought from actuarial companies.

There are several issues with the conventional referral process:

- *Perception*: At best, referral guidelines are viewed as educational checklists by PCPs, and at worst as intrusive "cookbook medicine" that damages their autonomy.

- *Validity*: If a healthy, low-risk patient seeks a colonoscopy because their neighbor just got diagnosed with colorectal cancer, that's the service they want, not what they need. Sometimes patients demand specialist referrals, mistaking them for better care. In such cases, PCPs want the payer to be the one to deny the request, in order to mitigate the risk of being perceived as gatekeepers.

- *Coverage*: On the other hand, referrals are sometimes made for treatment that may be medically indicated but is not covered by insurance company.

- *Authorization complexity*: Some referrals will be to specialists within a PCP's own medical group, obviating the need to check on insurance coverage. However, other cases will require familiarity with the specifics of various insurance plans and companies. The details of preferred and contracted networks are often so complicated that the ordinary PCP needs cheat sheets, administrative personnel, and/or management companies to sort them out.

- *Follow-up*: Referrals result in a continuous back-and-forth communication between providers. For example, say a PCP decides to refer a patient to a surgeon. The PCP can assume that after running tests and examining the patient, it's the surgeon who will finally decide if surgery is necessary. Knowing that, what should the PCP authorize in the referral? Should it be the surgery, or surgery and all other required services, or just the initial examination by the surgeon? It's not uncommon to have multiple follow-up referrals.

- *Inconvenience*: Patients end up being the usual conduit for referrals. They make the additional trips or phone calls to pick up or deliver referrals, get updates, or to figure out insurance coverage.

An HIE-level tool to manage referrals can create a common, patient-based view of all the different referral communication threads. Using a tool like that, any physician in the HIE network can find the right provider and carry on the back-and-forth of referral messages without faxes, phone calls, or EHR interfaces. Features like receipt acknowledgement, recipient inactivity alerts, EHR inbox integration, real-time insurance authorization, and instant scheduling can make the clinician's referral workflow smoother.

From an administrator's point of view, knowing the referral patterns and performing audits are the key needs. Knowing what categories of patients are being referred out of the HIE network (i.e. "Leakage Report") is the main metric closely followed by HIEs. That's because it represents a missed revenue opportunity; especially if that particular referred-for service already exists within the HIE network. No wonder referrals workflow is a feature that all vendors feel the urge to claim.

Care Management

The coverage of an HIE goes across multiple care organizations, spanning multiple visits for every patient. That comprehensive view provides a unique opportunity to systematically identify and address unmet care needs. That's what care management alerts can do at an individual patient level. For example, for a long-standing diabetic who comes in for flu, the system can remind the physician of an overdue HbA1c test (which should be regularly done for diabetics). Such proactive monitoring can reduce care gaps and improve patient experiences as well as outcomes.

Risk-stratification by the Analytics Layer of an HIE can identify a subset of patients who can benefit from a particular service or intervention. The Presentation Layer then displays them in the appropriate workflow as a module.

On the simpler end, the presentation could just be a *feature*. Like a color-coded patient list, a non-obtrusive message box, an alert bar in the LPR, or a daily/weekly automated e-mail message.

More complex presentation could mean a dedicated population-level *module* that allows clinical users to view their entire patient panel, filter them based on custom criteria, create batch or individual orders, and generate report or task lists. A detailed module like that is the territory of Population Health Management (or PHM, explained in section 5.6) technology, not really HIEs. But it's an overlap area nevertheless, so partnerships between PHM and HIE vendors make complete sense in this regard.

The care management value proposition is most utilized in primary care settings and used for patients with (or at risk of) major chronic clinical conditions like asthma, diabetes, and heart disease.

Health Summaries

The central function of an HIE's Presentation Layer is displaying a patient's record based on information gathered from the community.

Using an underlying data model, HIEs can harmonize the clinical and financial data from multiple sources on-demand to create a useful "Health Summary." They contain the common denominator of pertinent information that would (should) be valued by all HIE users. Also known as "Patient Summary" or "Visit Summary," it contains data like medications, problems, allergies, lab results, and immunizations. Such data is of obvious use in helping health professionals provide unscheduled care like emergency room visits. It can also be beneficial in planned medical care situations like when patients move to a new location or change insurances.

The standard(s) with which these summaries have been exchanged have evolved over past few years. The initial standard called Continuity of Care Record (CCR) was created by the American Society for Testing & Materials (ASTM) more than a decade ago.[34] Around the same time, another industry organization, Health Level Seven International (HL7.org), developed their own standard called Clinical Document Architecture (CDA). Politics and arguments ensued and (to make a long story short) CCR was merged into CDA format to create a new HL7 standard called the Continuity of Care document (CCD). In 2012, Stage 2 of the Meaningful Use program redirected attention to a superset of CCD called Consolidated CDA (C-CDA). Even though C-CDA was legitimized as an integral part of federal regulation, it hasn't really taken off in the real world.

If you are not cross-eyed with standards and acronyms yet, consider this: HL7 has been developing another standard since 2012, called Fast Healthcare Interoperability Resources (FHIR, pronounced as "fire"). Most people are very optimistic about the new standard and its viability. FHIR is modular at its core, based on RESTful web services that make it easy to build small adapters to cover just the needed data. It's early days for FHIR, so adoption in the real world is low but hopes are high for market-wide interoperability deliverance.

4.4.3. Key Use Cases

Viewing the HIE's information is akin to looking at the forest, not the tree. In everyday life, the healthcare system tends to be transactional in nature, focusing on a patient's current visit and current problem. That's why most providers are predisposed to be closer to the tree (i.e. current visit), and not know much about the forest (like care history and prevention).

Now that we've discussed the presentation layer from a functional perspective, it's befitting to end with an overview of the "forest-view" capability of an HIE's LPR.

- *Emergency*: Care providers in an emergency care situation find LPR valuable because it provides critical information for the patient that would likely otherwise be unavailable, especially in cases where the patient is unable to interact. LPR can prove beneficial even before patients reach the ED. EMS professionals can look up patient data while the patient is being transported to the ED and perform more personalized interventions.

- *Primary Care*: PCPs are the consistent front-line in care delivery for most patients and always need to gather background on what happened elsewhere (like Emergency Department admissions, abnormal lab results, or missed referral appointments). Without an HIE, the usual ways to inform PCPs would be what patients disclose themselves or faxed reports (which require a formal request). With an LPR, the primary care provider can look this up themselves, on-demand. They can also "subscribe" to the health event updates for their patients (all or specific ones) to have a continuous oversight and provide proactive care as needed. This is the "Patient Event Subscription" feature: a nifty value proposition that only HIEs are truly capable of delivering.

- *Specialists*: Like a PCP, the specialist is also looking for relevant background information from validated sources instead of relying on short referral notes or a patient's self-volunteered information. The main difference is that a specialist would probably be interested in only the subset of data that is relevant to their specialty. The referral management functionality described before gives more background around this.

- *Care Management*: With the resurgence of population-centric views of care, today's organizations are employing dedicated "Care Managers" who help manage difficult patients with multiple issues by reaching out periodically. This extra layer of personnel support keeps an eye on the at-risk population and reduces need for emergencies and hospitalization. The LPR would be the tool of choice for them because it gives an overarching view of what is going on with a patient, highlighting any gaps in care that are difficult to spot in visit-focused records.

4.5. Service Layer

Service-Oriented Architecture (SOA) is a set of design principles for designing, building, and maintaining software applications that are aligned with business processes (instead of hardware). The goal of this approach is to create an architecture that abstracts consumers of services from the applications and technology infrastructure that deliver the services.

The Service Layer of an HIE applies these SOA principles to modularize functionality and expose key processes that can be used by other systems. Popular HIE services examples are: searching for a patient, generating a patient list, and retrieving documents for a patient. Integrations done in this abstracted way simplify implementation and maintenance for all stakeholders. Besides facilitating integration, this layer fuels a viable business model: metered APIs for these services can help an HIE monetize its value as a platform.

HIE services are of two types: internal and external. Internal services abstract functionality mostly for self-consumption, making the whole HIE design easier to maintain and grow. External services are mostly for third-party applications and systems (like EHRs and PACS) to connect with an HIE and execute business transactions. Neither category is absolute, because once a service has been created, it may be used in an internal or external context. Let's discuss some examples of each type.

4.5.1. Internal HIE Services

Provider Directory Services

Payer and provider organizations have many reasons to keep a pulse on their network because it continuously changes characteristics and composition. For example:

- Contracts keep evolving due to re-negotiation of existing deals or creation of new ones.

- Processing and paying claims requires keeping up with rates, payment terms, and remittance information.

- Insured patients need an accurate directory of clinicians that they can browse and search.

A Provider Directory addresses this constant need for an up-to-date set of information for each physician. It contains attributes such as location, phone, gender, fax, insurances accepted, specialty, licensing, privileges, and hospital affiliation. As the source of truth for clinician identification, it enables other applications to manage authentication and authorizations. Some states actually consider directories to be public utilities and use them for things like Drug Enforcement Agency (DEA) registration, statewide claims databases, fraud databases, and registries.

HIEs can host a regional Provider Directory and provide the needed administration of user accounts, privileges, roles, and relationships. That would include the critical process of identity-proofing individuals, which can range from simple Active Directory (Microsoft's directory service standard) integration to elaborate, paper-document based verifications. Provider Directory Services expose the key capabilities of populating, managing, and accessing this kind of directory data.

Consent Management Services

If you think that a patient's consent is a simple Boolean flag to be stored in a table somewhere, think again. Consent is a surprisingly complex multifactorial concept that is mired in vague laws with regional variations. Consider the following examples of what needs to be factored into formatting consent information:

- Consent can be of *different types*: consent to disclose information, consent to access information.

- Consent can be given at *different levels*: physician, group, region, state, HIE.

- Consent can have *different implementations*: full opt-in, full opt-out, opt-in with restrictions, opt-out with exceptions.

- Consent can have *different workflows*, like some that override consent (called "break-the-glass" functionality), and let providers access information in case of emergency.

- Consent is governed by *different laws* that vary by state: For example, in NY a minor (under 18 years) can given informed consent to receive certain reproductive mental health services regardless of their parent's consent.[35] So the consent management software has to not only track the parental consent but also the child's birth date and procedure/diagnosis, and reconcile them constantly.

- Other thorny questions: Time range (can/should consent be retrospectively applied? How to handle reports that have been produced before patient chooses to opt-out?), Public health considerations (does the state own information about critical communicable diseases irrespective of individual consent?), What should it default to if consent is unknown (consider it opt-in? out? restricted?), How to handle conflicts between the systems that claim to have different consent for the same person, etc.

All these nuances need to be reflected in a software solution that tackles consent for any health-related enterprise. With their broad reach, HIEs are in a unique position to be a hub for consent management. States and regional organizations can use Consent Management Services from an HIE to implement their policies and provide more effective control over patient data.

Terminology services

Representing clinical information in a machine-understandable way is a fundamental requirement of digital health applications. Controlled terminologies convert unstructured, narrative clinical input into symbols that can have a consistent meaning when interpreted by different computer systems (thus enabling *semantic* interoperability).

Medical data standards started appearing in the 1970s and proliferated as hundreds of independent attempts were made at creating localized controlled terminologies. In the following years it became clear that having multiple standards was hindering, not promoting, the original goal of efficient interoperability. By 1986, the unmanageable proliferation prompted the U.S. National Library of Medicine to create a thesaurus called the Unified Medical Language System (UMLS, nlm.nih.gov/research/umls) to help translation amongst terminologies.

The three most-often-used terminologies are: International Classification of Diseases (ICD), Current Procedural Terminology (CPT), and the Systematized Nomenclature of Medicine Clinical Terms (SNOMED CT). Automated mapping and translation between different formats is a much-needed service, and as before, HIEs tend to be in a great position for offering it to others.

Terminology Service can allow cross-mapping of disparate codes and descriptors into a normalized common standard. That way, users get consistent representations of clinical data regardless of variations in the original data source. The underlying capabilities are usually provided by a partner, and the three market leading companies in this space are: Apelon.com, HealthLanguage.com, and Intelligent Medical Objects, Inc (e-imo.com).

Security Services

Like any true software platform, HIEs need to provide an abstraction layer that can insulate its participants from security-related implementation details. Here are some examples of such services:

- *Authentication* Service (identity verification): Ensure that a person, organization or application is correctly claiming the identity provided. Provider Directory Services, as described above, can be considered a type of such authentication.

- *Authorization* Service (access control): Ensures that the user accesses protected resources in accordance with the permissions granted.

- *Audit* Service: Defines and collects relevant system events and data as determined by policy, regulation, or risk profiles.

- *Encryption* Service: Protects all data with at-rest and in-transit encryption.

- *De-identification* Service: Removes (anonymization) or replaces (pseudonymization) the individually-identifiable information from a health record.

The various standards that help create the architecture for such an enterprise-grade security framework already exist in the technology industry. For example, SAML (Security Assertion

Markup Language) for authentication, XACML (eXtensible Access Control Markup Language) for access control, and RBAC (Role-Based Access Control) for user management.

It all may sound geeky and complicated, but these services are the building blocks that decrease application development, administration, and maintenance costs. They are key to scaling up an HIE-based ecosystem.

4.5.2. External HIE Services

Direct Messaging Service

We discussed the fundamentals of a "Directed Exchange" briefly in section 4.1. Anatomy of an HIE. That model is based on a unique public-private collaboration called the Direct Project (directproject.org), sponsored in 2010 by ONC to develop specifications, services and policies for secure communication in healthcare. The resulting standard (called "Direct") is meant to be used just like e-mail: to push messages securely between any two stakeholders in healthcare.

At its core, Direct protocol requires the message body and any attachments to be encrypted using Public Key Infrastructure and X509 Certificates. This level of encryption enables Direct-compliant messages to meet HIPAA requirements for protecting patient information. Meaningful Use program requirements encouraged the use of Direct-compliant products, but Direct never got the traction its promoters had hoped for.

One of the big problems was that the protocol didn't come with a viable plan for creating directories, i.e. lists of all addresses one can send a message to. Direct standard turned out to be a hastily-mandated transport protocol without much thought given to the originating and destination endpoints. There are currently some half-baked attempts to create public-private governance around it (like DirectTrust.org), but no real reason to be optimistic.

Regardless of chaotic underpinnings, there is plenty of money and attention still being given to the Direct Messaging capability. Most of the big-name EHRs in the market today have built or partnered on a Direct Messaging solution. Because most HIEs are funded with government money, this regulation-driven standard becomes a high priority for them by default.

In fact, some industry analysts have started calling out a subclass of HIEs as "MicroHIEs" because all they do is Direct Messaging. These HIEs are essentially state-sponsored secure e-mail inbox providers that provide the first few months of service free in hopes of getting entrenched as a replacement for fax-based communication. It hasn't worked out that way so far, and adoption numbers are abysmally low.

IHE Services

Formed in 1998, Integrating the Healthcare Enterprise (IHE) is an industry group with the goal of promoting interoperability amongst imaging and healthcare information systems. IHE's output is in the form of "Integration Profiles" (ihe.net/profiles) that are information models describing aspects like workflow context, systems involved, and specific standards used. Currently there are 122 IHE profiles in various stages of development across multiple clinical domains. The Health IT vendor community has always displayed strong support for IHE. Since 2000, various vendors have assembled and collaborated at the annual HIMSS conference "Connectathons" to demonstrate the way their products can interoperate using IHE profiles.

All HIEs offer services complying with IHE profiles to promote plug-and-play integration. Below are three key IHE profiles:

- *Patient Identifier Cross Referencing (PIX)*: Handles identity management by cross-referencing the patient identifiers created by local clinical systems at individual facilities.

- *Patient Demographics Query (PDQ)*: Provides a way to discover patients based on their demographic information such as name, date of birth, and phone number.

- *Cross-enterprise Document Sharing (XDS.b)*: Enables sharing of documents between healthcare facilities through a common document registry and a document repository.

Health Summary Services

This service allows an external entity to request patient information from the HIE. Requests can be for a single consolidated "Health Summary" document (described earlier in section 4.4. Presentation Layer) or specific parts of it like problems, allergies, and medications. for a given patient. Filters such as date-range and consent can also be applied while accessing this information. Done correctly, this service exemplifies what true market interoperability would look like: standardized health information output available as an API for anyone to create innovative solutions with.

Federal Services

HIE can be an efficient intermediary through which government agencies exchange information with multiple regional hospitals and health systems. For example, the Social Security Administration (SSA) routinely needs medical records for disability determination of the roughly 15 million applications they process every year. Conventional methods of collecting that information are labor-intensive (phone calls, faxes, and paper mail) and stretch the average processing time into months. Instead, requesting and receiving the needed health information electronically allows SSA to decrease operating costs and wait times for applicants.

Similarly, military service members and their families are transient populations that often change location and care providers. HIEs can enable better care coordination between the civilian and military providers in a region, as well as give the service member a consistent portal to access all their health information.

Trusted connections to such national-level agencies are complicated. There are several bureaucratic steps, certifications, and security requirements that make the task non-trivial and it is very unlikely that a smaller individual organization can sustain these prerequisites. Which is why HIEs are the perfect regional intermediaries to make it all work.

4.6. Analytics Layer

An HIE is built to receive and aggregate the health information output of all its participants. Their architecture gives HIEs a default ability to merge clinical and financial data. It all starts with the Data Layer that creates the needed normalized and consolidated information views, as we discussed before. But the real magic happens in the Analytics Layer, which hosts the data models and applications needed for generating useful insights.

The key components of an HIE's Analytics Layer includes data models, ETL (Extract, Transform, and Load) tools, a rules authoring environment, and pre-built data marts for reporting requirements like PQRS, HEDIS, ACO, and MU. But let's steer away from discussing *how* the Analytics Layer works, because that information can be easily found in any industry-agnostic resource around Business Intelligence and applied to healthcare. Instead, we'll focus on *what* this layer gets used for and why we need it.

Data-driven analyses can serve two different perspectives based on the timeframes in question—retrospective and prospective. The former looks at past data to give historical insights, while the latter looks forward and attempts to predict the possibilities of specific outcomes. Either of those two perspectives can be applied to the categories of analytics described below. The intention of this list is to exemplify the kinds of insights expected from an HIE ecosystem.

Infrastructure Analytics

Exchange administrators need to keep an eye on who is using the applications, how are they using them, and how well the exchange is operating overall. It's useful to track metrics like usage patterns, query-response times, application states, security policies compliance, and volume of transactions. Real-time reporting and periodic audits around such metrics are important for smooth day-to-day operations of an exchange.

Clinical Analytics

The legacy of reporting and analytics in healthcare has been providing insights into billing. Clinical Analytics is the evolutionary extension that focuses on analyses of data gathered during delivery of medical care.

Clinicians and administrators have many reasons to perform these kinds of analyses: checking compliance with a medical protocol, identifying potential gaps in care, finding patients eligible for care-management programs, creating network-wide registries, etc. Understanding care delivery from this perspective can reduce costs and improve quality of service, creating a fundamental impact on the business.

Examples for Clinical Analytics are jargonistic and discomfortingly granular to most non-healthcare reviewers. For example, figuring out the percentage of women who receive recommended antibiotics within an hour before the start of their cesarean section. Or the percentage of patients with a diagnosis of HIV/AIDS for whom a syphilis screening was performed. Or the number of patients with a diagnosis of ischemic stroke who were administered heparin medication by the end of hospital day two. The list of such measures is expectedly daunting because the permutations of care interventions across all health conditions are countless. Nevertheless, a fantastic starting list of such measures

Quality Reporting System (PQRS) program, and the Healthcare Effectiveness Data and Information Set (HEDIS) reporting.

Most HIE vendors have pre-built templates and reporting workflows that align with such regulations. Regulatory function shows up as prominent feature in most sales pitches. This category does have some overlap with reports generated within Public Health and Clinical Analytics.

Ad-hoc Analytics

Predefined reports can only partially cover analytics need and custom insights are always needed. Advanced users often demand to explore the HIE datastore on their own so that they can drill down into their specific areas of interest. That's where designing custom queries through an intuitive, drag-and-drop interface comes in handy. Most customers that use this HIE capability are large institutions that can pay the heavy price tag for Ad-hoc Analytics licenses.

5

Emerging Areas

5.1. Overview

Systemic changes have happened before in healthcare, but never so many nearly simultaneously. Major shifts in regulations, technology capabilities, and consumer expectations inside and outside the healthcare industry made 2010–2015 a watershed period.

So far in this book, we've discussed healthcare's transformation as it relates to the broad strokes of EHR and HIE technologies. This section is dedicated to other trends and areas that have the potential to create tectonic shifts in the industry and provide fertile grounds for next-generation companies.

Bill Gates once said "We always overestimate the change that will occur in the next two years and underestimate the change that will occur in the next ten." Similarly, not everything mentioned in this section may have the same impact or time-to-maturity in health. As in most of this book, the coverage is intended to be exemplary and not comprehensive.

5.2. Telehealth

It's here. Finally.

Telemedicine is a perfect illustration of the famed Gartner Hype Cycle.[36] Developed by the advisory firm Gartner, Inc., the Hype Cycle provides a graphical and conceptual presentation of the lifecycle of emerging technologies through five phases.

The "Technology Trigger" for telemedicine happened in the late 1960s with government-funded research, and finally became practical in the 1980s with the advent of personal computing. By the mid-1990s, several hyped pilots were in motion and a "Peak of Inflated Expectations" had been achieved. In the early 2000s telemedicine began its slide down into the "Trough of Disillusionment." Stumbling pilots, legal anxiety, and poor adoption led most to doubt the return on investments in telemedicine technology.

All that has changed in the last five years. The combination and near-synchronous rising trends of smartphones, internet connectivity, cheap sensors, and payment reform have created the needed force to push telemedicine onto the "Slope of Enlightenment." It has also gathered a broader, better name: "Telehealth." Now few doubt its viability and there is widespread awareness of its benefits, risks, and applications.

Here are the specific changes that prove that this paradigm shift is here to stay:

- The government thinks it's legitimate. In January 2015, CMS issued a new provider reimbursement code (CPT 99490) for non–face-to-face health care services for patients who have chronic medical conditions. It allows an approximately $40 payment for 20 minutes of *non-face-to-face* chronic care management (CCM) services per patient every month. That non-face-to-face part is what legitimizes telehealth as something the government thinks is worth paying for. The payment may sound trivial, but do the math: the average PCP has around 1,500–2,000 patients under care annually. Even if only 500 of those are eligible for CCM, there is an annual payment of $20,000 per physician on the table for remotely monitoring and interacting with patients. There are catches to this deal, of course. Patients have to explicitly agree to be in the CCM program and shell out a monthly $8 co-pay. This is the start of a torrent of federal money that will germinate the long-sown seeds of telehealth, just like what the HITECH Act did for the EHR industry.

- Big vendors and deals are emerging. The top four players (Teladoc.com, MDLive.com, AmericanWell.com, and DoctoronDemand.com) have continued double-digit growth and multi-million-dollar funding. Teladoc has blazed the path and even went public in early 2015. The official bonds these companies have formed with health insurers is what really underscores future viability. Multiple deals have been struck with big names like United Healthcare, WellPoint, Aetna, Cigna, and CVS Health to offer telehealth as either as an optional-and-charged service or as an included-and-free service. When traditional insurers start offering telehealth, it's time to pay attention.

- Regulatory forces are moving fast. In April 2014, the Federation of State Medical Boards (FSMB) adopted a model policy to guide state licensure boards in evaluating the appropriateness of using telehealth in care delivery.[37] 2015 saw more than 200 Telehealth-related bills introduced in 42 states.[38] Medicaid programs in almost all states (49 actually) and the District of Columbia already have some coverage for Telehealth. In June 2015, the Texas Medical Board stated their disapproval of virtual visits with physicians who have not previously seen patients in-person and ruled that a provider-patient relationship can't be established remotely. Dallas-based Teladoc, in turn, sued the Texas Medical Board for being anti-competitive. The analysis of all this legal wrangling shouldn't predict winners or losers. A more important takeaway is that there is continuous movement. The legal landscape is shifting, and evolving faster than ever before.

If care interactions are not restricted to a physical location, the aspects of such virtualization open up many chances to create viable businesses. Existing online technology infrastructure around audio, video, mobile, security, payment, reviews, marketplaces, and on-demand services will all need to be customized for telehealth applications. In that sense, healthcare is now starting to experience the early years of ecommerce and online transactions. Emerging services like Telepathology, teledermatology, telepsychiatry, and telestroke will transform their conventional, real-world parent fields.

Wearables

The popularization of wearable devices is a trend that further proves the ongoing maturity of the remote monitoring phenomenon, albeit from a non-clinical perspective. Innovations from Fitbit, Misfit, Garmin, Apple, and others have helped create a mass awareness (and acceptance) of wearing sensors that detect some physiological metric(s) about the user's body. Deriving continuous insights from the gathered data and connecting services (running coach, for example) is going mainstream too.

Imagine the traditional medical device industry at one end of a spectrum and the consumer electronics industry at another. Players at the ends of that range are constantly yearning to stretch their product appeal toward the opposite side. Medical device makers are trying to create more apps and mobile add-ons to help them appear consumer-friendly. For example, take the surge in smartphone-compatible glucometers. On the flip side, retail players like Samsung and Apple are getting serious about the health-related value propositions of their devices. That's why one can find banal activity monitors now marketed with heart-health buzzwords.

With the medical establishment opening up to Telehealth and consumers understanding the concept of remote monitoring at the same time, the future is getting exciting. Before long, a significant quantity of medically-relevant data will be collected outside of clinical settings, often before any medical need arises.

5.3. Services

Mammoth categories like EHR (handling all local clinical workflows) and HIE (connecting all healthcare organizations in a community) are reaching a point where it's impossible for vendors to deliver satisfactorily on everything. That's why the players in these categories have broad functional parity, rather than excellence in any one aspect. Alongside this bloatware landscape are the green shoots of some startups doing few services, and doing them right.

It makes sense that a company that has a laser focus on nailing one or two aspects will end up creating a superior offering. Here are some example spaces that have started to emerge as good candidates for "externalization," i.e. done by a few dedicated vendors and utilized by all others.

Scheduling services

We've all experienced the unpleasant surprise of finding out that the first available appointment with your doctor of choice is weeks or months away. Match-making between the patient and doctor's schedule has always been a manual process, usually done as a conversation with the front-desk staff. Meanwhile, other industries have realized the efficiencies of allowing customers to self-schedule their interactions. OpenTable.com was founded in 1998 to schedule restaurant reservations and sold to Priceline.com for $2.6 billion in 2014. Healthcare scheduling startups have started growing roots in the last few years.

Most notably, Zocdoc.com has forged the path, turbo-charged by humongous funding ($223 million) and legendary backers (Vinod Khosla, Marc Benihoff, and Jeff Bezos). Since 2007 it has allowed patients to directly schedule their own non-emergency visits to clinics and doctor's offices. Similarly, Wisconsin-based MyHealthDirect.com provides white-labeled scheduling services for large health systems, insurers, and medical groups.

As we discussed previously, there are several young companies focusing on the topic of ED-related scheduling. For example, InQuicker.com, ERTexting.com, and ERExpress.com allow patients to find wait times and hold their place in virtual queues. That way patients with non-life-threatening medical conditions can stay at home until it's their turn to be seen. The operational benefits of having a smooth, just-in-time flow for such round-the-clock care delivery centers are huge from a staffing and customer satisfaction perspective.

A clinician's own scheduling is also a viable vertical that can be solved using the same underlying technology. Individual providers need to schedule their shifts and locations and then synchronize with their personal calendars that may be on external services like Google Calendar or iCloud. Plenty of nuances exist in that workflow, like shift swaps, didactic pairings, vacation request management, policy-based rules checks, duty-hour reports, and last-minute coverage changes. Furthermore, the challenges and complexities of scheduling in one clinical domain (like anesthesiology) may be different enough from another (like Emergency Medicine) to warrant different user experiences. Some examples of companies already doing well in this category are Amion.com and Lightning-bolt.com.

All these are optimistic signs that smart scheduling is soon going to be a modular service that can be embedded easily in any digital health offering.

Storage services

Cloud-based file storage-and-sync is another fundamental infrastructure service much needed in healthcare. Imagine if users could easily store sensitive health information in a HIPAA-compliant platform that is securely accessible from anywhere. That would take away some of the complexity in developing innovative healthcare applications.

Storage-as-a-service may sound simple but it has its share of challenges. Workflow integration is a big one. Stored information, like medications, needs to be readily accessible for partner applications that consume it (like the EHR's medication reconciliation module). Simple, elegant, and dependable APIs are needed for such workflow integrations. Another challenge is security and ownership of the data being handled. Does the account-holder have immutable ownership? The answer can be complicated by aspects like consent and regulations. For example, if the patient has anthrax (which is state-notifiable disease and a public health risk), the state owns the information irrespective of where or with whom it is stored.

The inherent complexities of healthcare information can be managed better if the information is accessible anytime, anywhere using a cloud storage service. Any platform that centralizes information and makes it available in an on-demand, device-independent way will be appreciated because it makes life easier for everyone involved.

Incumbent EHR and HIE vendors have no incentive to truly promote shared storage, irrespective of their public rhetoric. The market needs neutral parties to do the data arbitrage between patients, providers, and insurers. A high-profile example of such a vendor is Box.com, which announced its intention to enter the healthcare vertical in mid-2013. Since then it has forged ahead with an IPO, several vendor partnerships, and big-name hospital customers.

Directory services

An up-to-date, organized index is an important informational component everywhere—whether we are talking about music or shops in a mall. In healthcare, directories are most important in keeping track of patients and providers.

Patient directories are usually made by health systems and insurers to monitor visits and enrollments. An HIE's Master Patient Index (MPI) serves the same purpose. These directories can also be made for clinical reasons: to facilitate follow-ups and promote research, for example. The formal category name for such cases is "Clinical Registries."

Clinical Registries are focused lists of patients that share one or more common characteristic(s). The characteristic under review is usually a product (like patients exposed to the same drug or device), a service (like patients with the same procedure or encounter type) or a condition (same diagnosis). For example, an accurate list of patients with HIV has obvious importance for research. It becomes even more useful with detail like which antiretroviral drugs have been given to whom. Such a list would make it easier to pinpoint affected patients in case a drug was recalled for safety reasons (as actually happened in 2007 with Roche's drug Viracept).[39]

A non-enterprise analog to clinical registries are online patient communities. Today there are several web destinations where a common ailment or medical topic brings together a large number of individuals to create a virtual support network. Aside from Facebook groups, sites like PatientsLikeMe.com, MedHelp.org,

DailyStrength.org and SmartPatients.com are some examples of such niche patient networks.

Physician directories are just as promising. The conventional professional societies like the American Medical Association (AMA) and government databases like the NPI Registry (npiregistry.cms.hhs.gov) have been around as the traditional sources of this information. Now startups are emerging with private, more accurate virtual network directories. The three largest physician-only online networks are Sermo.com, Doximity.com, and QuantiaMD.com. They verify identity credentials and offer secure online communication, collaboration, and career-development for their users. Some startups have taken a different approach by aggregating various available public data sets to create web destinations that enable searching, browsing, and reviewing physicians. For example, DocSpot.com, Vitals.com, and HealthGrades.com.

The point here is that accurate directories of individual patients and physicians are incredible utilities and there is more than one way of creating them. Once a worthwhile directory exists, other systems can simply use that instead of recreating their own version.

Perhaps current dominating social mega-networks like Facebook or LinkedIn will end up serving as de facto directories for all contexts, including health. Don't bet on that though, because past a certain size, generic networks run the risk of imploding under their own weight. The crowd becomes so large and diffuse that it decreases the quality of individual, health-related interactions.

Communication services

The modern world has long incorporated e-mail and text as ubiquitous modes of communication, but healthcare seems to be mired in phone calls, pagers, faxes and paper mail. E-mail has trickled into some scenarios (e.g. visit reminders) but it still can't include sensitive information like lab results. Physician-physician and physician-patient communication is still stuck in the 20th century.

Administrators in any hospital, clinic, or payer organization would love to have a mobile-friendly secure e-mail and/or texting service for their verified users. Currently their options are to either use what comes as a part of enterprise software like EHRs (which is restricted to explicitly on-boarded users only) or throw caution to the wind and allow non-secure public services (like Apple iMessage or Google GMail). Neither solution works well in the end, which is why communication is a great focus area for stand-alone offerings.

Enterprise-focused software vendors like TigerText.com, Datamotion.com, PatientSafeSolutions.com, PerfectServe.com, Voalte.com, and Vocera.com are creating multi-modal platforms that make it easier for healthcare stakeholders to communicate with each other, both inside and outside clinical settings.

Elsewhere, the overall mobile communication market keeps evolving continuously. For example, take the developments around wearable form factors like Apple Watch, self-destructing messages like SnapChat, and image sharing communities like Instagram. They may not be transferable to healthcare as-is, but these trends will surely end up influencing the kinds of communication solutions that are created for healthcare.

Pricing-related services

Healthcare pricing is notoriously arbitrary at best. For the same service, hospital prices can vary widely based on negotiations with individual insurance companies and large employers. The largest swing is in rates for self-paying individuals, which can sometimes exceed 1,000% of what others pay. The internal document where these prices are kept is called a "Charge Description Master" (CDM) or simply, the Chargemaster.

Google the term "Chargemaster" and the results will mostly be articles about these enigmatic and irrational price lists. Used as a facade for negotiating with insurers, a Chargemaster can inflict real damage on others. While most public and private health insurance companies negotiate the Chargemaster rates down, uninsured and out-of-network patients are billed the full price. If there ever was a science fiction written about hospital prices, Chargemaster would be the perfect name for the Dark Overlord character.

The indifference toward Chargemaster has been waning recently. With Obamacare's mandate for individual insurance and the popularity of high-deductible plans, even insured patients are starting to care about the prices they pay for healthcare. The state-level legislative view has been shifting too. Maryland started conducting a unique and ongoing price experiment in the late 1970s in which an independent commission set the rate structure for each hospital. All public and private payers then paid according to those fixed rates. On October 1, 2015, Massachusetts became the first state to require that insurers and hospitals make real-time cost information publicly available.

Going forward, services that offer comparison shopping, fair price estimates, out-of-pocket cost calculators, marketplaces, and drug price lists are great focus areas for startups. GoodRx.com, Pokitdok.com, and HealthSparq.com are some examples of companies already riding the trend. The most prominent price transparency company, CastLightHealth.com, went public in early 2014.

Many, many more services...

The above-mentioned areas are just the beginning of the service trend. More fundamental building blocks will surely emerge as time goes on and the market evolves inside and outside healthcare. Vendor-driven services in the form of APIs are also starting to emerge, albeit often in poorly documented and rigid forms. For example, Cerner, AllScripts, AthenaHealth, Optum, and Kaiser have all publicly announced "open" APIs and/or app stores.

5.4. Analytics

Analytics is a general term for the process of using technology to answer questions. The tools and techniques for doing so have long been evolving across industries. Predictive modeling, alerts, dashboards, query mechanisms, standard reporting, and ad hoc reporting are not exclusive to healthcare, but greatly applicable nevertheless. It wouldn't be worthwhile to detail these methods here because that information is easy to find on the web. Rather, let's talk about the overall need and application of analytics in healthcare.

For the longest time, a prominent intent of the Health IT industry was to digitize data creation and collection. That should sufficiently explain the meteoric rise of EHRs and HIEs in the last two decades. But as that goal starts being met, health organizations are grappling with the next question: "How can we make sense of all this digital data?" That's why in the last five years the category of data analytics has gained popularity amongst healthcare vendors and customers alike.

At the forefront of this data deluge are big health systems that were the pioneers of digitization. Kaiser Permanente, for example, formally completed its Epic EHR adoption journey in 2010 after seven years of implementation and an estimated $4 billion price tag. It's estimated that Kaiser creates two terabytes of data every day. Not surprisingly, stakeholders are now feeling a bit lost in the information avalanche and turning to analytics technology for help. Take the example of two competing procedures called Vertebroplasty and Kyphoplasty. Both are used to treat painful vertebral compression fractures in the spinal column which are a common result of osteoporosis, but the medical literature seems to be inconclusive or insufficient in comparing their outcomes. Simultaneous Bilateral Cataract Surgery (SBCS) vs. single-eye cataract surgery is another example of such a debate. In these cases, what should be the recommended standard procedure of choice at a given large hospital system? Analytics can provide an in-house evidence base to answer that question by looking at the demographics, clinical profile, and recovery patterns of the patient population.

Beside rising customer need, market conditions are also getting favorable for analytics. Regulatory changes like Accountable Care and Meaningful Use have made it necessary to understand the risks inherent in the patient populations under care. Segmenting by risk and proactively managing the most vulnerable ones is the way to decrease costs. Lastly, the business need for complying with Meaningful Use attestation and quality-based reporting is clear.

The vendor lineup starts with industry-agnostic stalwarts like IBM.com, Xerox.com and SAS.com who are adept at selling to large accounts. Explicitly healthcare enterprise focused analytics players have existed for a few years too. For example, consider Optum.com, Medeanalytics.com, HealthCatalyst.com and MEDai.com. As expected, EHRs also offer some form of clinical and claims analytics tools natively. In the last five years, the number of startups in the health analytics area has skyrocketed.

What it entails

Roughly speaking, there are three categories of analytics in healthcare, based on the data being used: Clinical, Billing and Claims.

- *Clinical* dataset (like diagnoses, procedures, and lab results) is captured as a part of the actual care delivery. It's not very structured and tends to be scattered across departmental silos.

- *Billing* dataset consists of the claims sent by providers to the insurance companies. It closely tracks the services delivered and is transmitted as a group of structured transactions called the "EDI 837."

- *Claims* dataset makes up the actual payments by insurers, and is structured as "EDI 835" transactions.

All three of these datasets are misaligned and disconnected enough to yield different results when analyzed. Claims data in particular is often incorrect, delayed, and not detailed enough to be trusted. Regardless, it remains the popular basis for cost analysis and projections due to historical reasons. Most hyped is the clinical data because it has the potential to be closest to the truth. The capability to bring together clinical, billing, and claims data has long been the holy grail of healthcare analytics.

Anecdotally speaking, half of the cost for analytics initiatives is about getting the data. If data acquisition is faulty, it leads to a frustrating garbage-in-garbage-out ending. Results are much better if the quality and quantity issues of various incoming data streams have been worked out beforehand.

Not that big (yet)

Big data is the buzzword of choice for most analytics companies today. Roughly speaking, what makes data "big" is its size, the speed with which it is generated, and its heterogeneity. More important for startups, conventional data analysis tools can't get insights from big data, which requires an entirely new set of infrastructure and techniques.

The current data landscape in health seems more like "small" data, still capable of being handled with conventional approaches. Omics (discussed next) and patient-generated data are going to be the main drivers of big-data tools in healthcare. Nevertheless, let's try to remember that "liquid" data is a prerequisite for big data. We need to figure out viable interoperability and data-sharing before aspiring to big data insights.

5.5. Omics

Impending need to scale

The average file size of a text-only electronic medical record for a patient's phenotype (i.e. observable traits) is in the 0.5–1 MB range. Compare that with a typical radiology order (like X-ray, MRI, or CT) that yields multiple high-quality images of around 15–20 MB size each. Lossless compression techniques may bring file sizes down by about half, but there remains at least an order of magnitude jump in amount of data when images are included in medical data.

Enter genomics. The field of genomics explores how genetic variations affect susceptibility to diseases, and discovers new pathways and drug targets for treating genetic disease. The use of genetic testing for commonly used medications (like warfarin) can improve dosing and decrease adverse outcomes. Genomic research is done using a process called "sequencing" in which the order of nucleotides present in DNA or RNA molecules is determined. Around 2005, developments in the sequencing technology created the high-throughput "Next-Generation Sequencing" (NGS) technique which enabled processing a large number of samples in parallel.

Compared to the output of conventional sequencing (a few megabytes), whole genome sequencing files resulting from NGS are sized in hundreds of Gigabytes. Even analyzing only 1–2% of the whole genome (called "Exome Sequencing") still ends up generating files in the 5–10 GB range. That's a thousand-fold increase from medical image file sizes.

The real impact of genomics on Health IT is not a question of disk space. It's about the need to scale up the ability of healthcare systems to deal with the data deluge that is about to go mainstream. This evolving new body of information needs to be manipulated, analyzed, and integrated with patient care workflow tools.

Omics tsunami

Studying DNA (Genome) composition is just the start. Modern science has already established the relevance of looking at RNA (Transcriptome), proteins (Proteome), and small molecules (Metabolome). Looming on the horizon are a huge variety of genomics niches. Google the following terms to get a quick idea of what is coming: Epigenome, Microbiome, Variome, Interactome, Fluxome, and Regulome.

Delivering care based on such fine-tuned information has been called "Personalized Medicine," and it involves calibrating everything according to the individual molecular composition of a patient and supporting providers with the right evidence to help in decision-making. In his 2015 State of the Union address, President Obama announced the launch of a "Precision Medicine Initiative" (PMI) to enable advances in research, technology, and policies for a new era of medicine.

The changes needed

We'll also be entering a new era of health information systems as we deal with omics data. The good news is that this data, although massive in quantity, tends to be more structured than usual phenotypic data. However, the real challenge lies in integrating it with actual clinical care. Taking genomics as a reference, here are some issues already visible:

- There is no genomics-related detailed content in existing medical vocabularies. New terminologies, data models, and standards will be needed to interpret omics data consistently across systems.

- We need new applications that deploy omics insights where clinicians can easily use them in their decision-making. For example: displaying pharmacogenomic-based risks at time of writing a prescription. Specifically, showing whether the particular HIV mutations of the patient in question are associated with antiretroviral drug resistance or not.

- Traditional systems like EHRs are optimized for accessing information with temporary and individual values, like a patient's blood tests, as they relate to the current visit or problem. Genetic results, on the other hand, are lifelong and significant for family members too.

- The molecular diagnostics laboratories doing the genetic tests are not integrated with the EHR systems of healthcare organizations ordering them. Test results are currently delivered in formats (like PDF text) that can't simultaneously support discrete molecular information as well as clinical takeaways for the ordering physician.

- The complexity of genomic information warrants better aids for providers. Currently they have to parse through an overwhelming amount of resources to find the relevant evidence.

Tools like OMIM.org (a well-maintained catalog of human genes) and PharmGKB.org (information on the impact of genetic variation on drug responses) are creating the foundation for omics-enabled care. Startups are also making inroads into genome interpretation and clinical integration spaces. Some prominent examples are DNANexus.com, TuteGenomics.com. Syapse.com, Omicia.com, and Personalis.com.

5.6. PHM

Looking at the forest, not a tree

Most of the solutions and processes in healthcare are designed to serve sick individuals. They are made to be utilized in and around a service transaction taking place at a clinic or hospital. But once the transaction (i.e. visit) is over and the patient walks out of the facility door, what happens to them next remains mostly unknown. Until they show up sick again.

Population Health Management (PHM, or just Population Health) changes the traditional perspective for keeping a group of individuals healthy, and aims to avoid visits altogether. The central idea of PHM is that care should be about promoting health and preventing disease, rather than adeptly treating sickness.

Consider diabetes as an example. A poorly-controlled diabetic may have to endure fainting episodes, kidney failure, blindness, and stroke—all of which get prompt attention when the patient shows up in the ER or clinic with severe symptoms. The system pays a significant price for every such visit.

There are ways to *monitor* and *prevent* diabetes progression, however. Regular blood tests (HbA1c, Lipid profile, Blood glucose), eye and foot exams, and blood pressure recordings are some of the key metrics that help raise red flags in advance of a crisis. Similarly, there are interventions to prevent or slow diabetes, like lifestyle coaching, weight loss, and nutritional education. Even in non-clinical settings such as workplace health screenings or community events, there can be an opportunity to engage at-risk populations. Collectively, steps like these can offset potential future visits and costs to the system. An organization that creates a registry of their diabetic patient population, institutes a program with some of the steps described above, and measures success in terms of decreasing visits (i.e. costs), is practicing PHM.

Take a moment to reflect on the enormity of this shift. All the tools, processes, and people in the traditional health industry need to reconfigure from a *reactive* mode ("let's give the best care to this sick diabetic here") to a *proactive*, preventive one ("let's keep all diabetics healthy and at home as long as possible").

Collections of activities aimed at preventing disease and reducing actual visits were not reimbursable in the old fee-for-service model, but PHM rewards them. PHM is a change in perspective that refocuses an organization to the level of a forest, not the individual tree.

Needed underlying changes

The idea behind PHM is not new. Pioneering organizations like Kaiser Permanente have been running structured population care programs since the 1990s, albeit under other conceptual framework names like "Panel Management," "Disease Management," and "Care Management." Like PHM, these programs have involved addressing unmet chronic and preventive care needs. The program components were either embedded in the usual primary care or delivered by dedicated personnel.

In 2009, the term "Population Health" was legitimized with the enactment of HITECH, which included a cornerstone concept called the "Triple Aim." This concept called for the health system to pursue improvement in three dimensions simultaneously:

improving the individual experience of care, improving the health of populations, and reducing the per capita cost of healthcare. The following year, the Affordable Care Act provided a second boost for PHM. The sweeping reform tied provider payments with their adherence to spending targets specific to patient populations under their care. This change created an explicit need to recalibrate healthcare business and keep service utilization low across patient populations.

As expected, the next few years opened the floodgates for media, vendors, payers, and providers to monetize the "population" buzzword in every way possible. Everyone took what they were doing (or thinking of doing) and mapped it to Population Health. Today the realm of PHM solutions sprawls from the obviously visceral (like genetics, behavior, physiology) to the bafflingly abstract (social interaction, urban design, environment). The justification generally given is that any factor that may influence or reflect the health of a given population is part of the PHM story.

Maybe the expansive view of PHM is genuinely warranted and not just an opportunistic land-grab. Rather than talk about PHM's conceptual boundaries and limits, let's define it through what tactical changes are required in it. These execution elements can be broken down into three categories: tools, people, and processes.

Tools

A feature-rich technology toolkit is a necessary part of any PHM infrastructure. Some old-school care organizations have overlooked this and started executing on a PHM vision simply by adding personnel and tweaking existing processes. For example, if a new PHM contract with a local large employer adds 100,000 patients, an old-school care organization would hire 10 new employees as "Care Managers" to take care of that new population. That is not a viable way to scale the care to a larger pool.

Of course, people are important, but what really enables PHM scale is supporting technology infrastructure like:

- *Registry*: The first step of PHM is to identify the target population, be it a local geographic community, group of employees, or members of an insurance plan. But beyond being just an informational list of at-risk individuals, a PHM registry also pinpoints the gaps in care based on established protocols. For example, flagging a diabetic if they've not had HbA1c tested in the last six months, or haven't ordered strip refills in the last four months, or are more than 40 years old and missing a lipid-lowering drug in the last year of prescription history. Such flags are useful not only for unsolicited outreach but also "inreach," i.e. when patients arrive at a care facility for an unrelated reason.

- *Stratification Logic*: Individuals in dire need of PHM are often suffering from multiple ailments. Creating a cumulative score for all the care deficiencies is key to understanding the gravity of an individual case. For example, a diabetic with no prior eye exam is lower priority than one with uncontrolled BP and a missing HbA1c test result. Creating scorecards that can sort a patient population into graded levels helps prioritize PHM interventions.

- *Outreach Tools*: Once the target subpopulation is identified, reaching out to them may require various capabilities. Like sending a batch of secure e-mails, ordering a group of lab tests at a partner facility, or printing paper "Birthday Letters" to patients with gentle reminders to come in for preventive care. Systems that manage interaction channels like automated phone calls, text messages, social media, and mobile apps can be used to scale outreach to millions of patients.

- *Remote Monitoring*: Proactive outreach is great, but it shouldn't mean pinging the patient daily to ask how they are doing. Sensor technology has made cheap and reliable monitoring of physiological parameters possible (e.g. activity, sleep, BP, weight, SpO2, breathing, and temperature). Thanks to the ubiquity of mobile platforms, patients can do such basic monitoring on-demand or continuously from anywhere. All this progress enables care providers to keep an eye on patients between in-person visits.

- *Case Management*: The long-term process is more than e-mail blasts, phone calls, or sensor alerts. The people managing PHM need to keep track of individual patient responses and recalibrate accordingly. Case Management software helps in figuring out what works best for the given patient (i.e. personalization), allows the assigned care providers to make notes about the communications (like phone calls), and lets administrators oversee execution.

The list above is not complete but it does cover the key aspects of a PHM toolkit. Enthusiastic proponents of PHM tend to include more features like data acquisition solutions, care team communication, and reporting tools. We are better off discounting features that seem to be basic expectations of an enterprise system and not explicitly attributable to PHM.

People

Technology helps with scale but care providers are still the core of PHM. At the center of all population health work is a PCP directing the needed proactive care. Many of the basic outreach tasks (e.g. calling patients to remind them and setting up appointments) are appropriate for clerical staff. For more complicated tasks, like explaining medications or discussing lifestyle changes, ancillary clinical staff like nurses, pharmacists, and physician assistants can be pulled in when necessary.

There is a potential critique awaiting the staffing choices described above. Delegating tasks to other licensed staff like nurses may shift the clinical decision-making away from the PCP, potentially weakening their relationship with patients. That concern is unfounded. Effective staffing for serving millions of patients involves complex trade-offs, and concerns that the PCP doesn't get to be the face of all communication are of limited importance.

PCPs are the quarterbacks of PHM. Besides a rock-solid software tool, what they need most is a dedicated time to actually *do* PHM. For example, several 15-minute appointments slots every week or a day every month blocked off to look at the panel dashboard of all their patients, some of whom may not have presented for care. Speaking of dedicated time, everyone on the PHM team needs time to identify patients with the greatest needs, gather information, and communicate with patients and physicians.

As the PHM market explodes, the jobs within population health are getting more explicitly marketed. Here are the main categories of responsibilities in the PHM team and the creative titles associated with them:

- *Doing basic logistical tasks* like phone calls, check-ins, scheduling, simple interviews, and surveys. Examples of related titles: Registration Staff, Social Worker, Patient Navigator, and Community Resource Specialist.

- *Delivering individualized preventive care services* like periodic assessments, counseling, education, and overall care

191

coordination. The people responsible are usually clinically-licensed (e.g. nurses, pharmacists) with special training relevant to PHM like motivational interviewing and behavior modification coaching. They play an almost-independent role in managing care for high-risk patients by performing tasks like ordering routine tests, titrating medication dosage, and providing self-management support. Titles are usually various combinations of: Care Manager, Care Coordinator, Case Manager, Clinical Pharmacist, and Care Transitions Coach.

- *Helping collect, interpret, and present data* related to PHM. This support staff includes the usual cadre of Business Analyst, Project Manager, and Data Scientist roles. Additional, more pointed titles can include Manager of Population Health Analytics, or Director of Population Health.

- *Administration and oversight* of PHM activities. This includes corporate-level work like setting strategy, managing partner relationships, negotiating contracts, ensuring compliance, and managing budgets. It's safe to say that having an MD (or at least a clinical background) is a mandatory price of admission to this select club. Many conventional executive roles like VP of Clinical Services, Chief Medical Officer, or CIO often have their authority spill over into this PHM territory. Newer titles range from the hyperbolic "Chief Transformation Officer" (as many organizations rightly feel that PHM is a business transformation), to the more direct "VP of PHM."

Processes

Becoming PHM-centric is a culture change that needs to be managed as people and tools are being put into place. For example, if the workforce feels that PHM tasks are added extra work, adoption will suffer regardless of new technology or additional hires. That's why it is vital to create clear processes that fit in well with existing workflows.

Below are some examples of PHM workflows that require formalized processes. That means figuring out who does what, where, and how, in addition to the usual overhead of contingency planning, compliance auditing, and reporting for the new processes.

- Proactively generating the list of targeted patients and identifying their care gaps.

- Periodically reviewing that info with the care team and getting necessary approvals for next steps.

- Performing the agreed-upon steps and documenting their progress.

- Collecting and documenting patient vitals during visit, identifying and flagging alerts for providers.

- Sending after-visit summary, instructions, education materials, and setting up future appointments for patients.

It's easy to describe the PHM process through the example of a clinician pulling up a list of targeted patients and poring over it in a dedicated time, figuring out next steps in each person's care. But population care can also happen in concert with every patient visit. Before a physician walks into the exam room, the ideal PHM system would inform them on what to discuss with the patient. The resulting conversations can change the course of the patient's health. For example: "Looks like you are due for a flu shot," or "Let's talk about colorectal cancer screening at your age" is population care, one patient at a time.

When it comes to PHM, most large health systems tend to do everything in-house. But a significant number of them choose to contract PHM activities out to "Disease Management" (DM) companies. These companies took off in the 1990s by providing integrated care for a handful of diseases like diabetes, asthma, and heart failure in chronically ill patients. On behalf of their providers, they checked in with patients regularly, nagging them to take their pills and watch what they eat. The DM industry flourished and gradually expanded into other conditions like obesity, back pain, and depression. The range of services offered expanded as well. Today DM companies run wellness programs, coaching services, and incentive offerings, among many other things.

The real ROI on outsourced DM remains fuzzy because of the multiple variables involved. Still, these companies provide a practical option for care organizations to start PHM with the least impact to their internal care delivery workflow process.

5.7. Speech Recognition

Today voice-to-text technology is widely available on consumer devices, thanks to companies like Apple and Google. But Speech Recognition (SR, also known as Voice Recognition) was one of the rare tech-adoption examples where healthcare was ahead of the general market. Radiologists were experimenting with SR as early as the 1990s, in an effort to reduce turnaround time in reporting results.

SR is reshaping the dated "Medical Transcription" industry, which traditionally outsourced a clinician's audio message to a remote person for interpretation and typing. Out-of-the-box solutions like MModal.com, or the more expensive Dragon Medical (by Nuance.com) are replacing medical dictation. The market reality now is such that SR is neither a differentiator for an EHR nor restricted to radiology. Although not yet perfected, it's already a widely-accepted alternative to typed documentation for clinical users.

In the near future, the act of digitally capturing a clinical narrative will be as easy as having a conversation. No longer needing to fiddle with a keyboard, clinicians will probably get back to making eye contact with patients once more. Frictionless data capture will make workflows more efficient and increase satisfaction for everyone involved.

5.8. NLP

The expressions in any given language contain underlying concepts that convey the meaning (semantics) of how people, places, or things interact with each other. Acting synergistically with Speech Recognition, Natural Language Processing (NLP) allows machines to encode such semantics of natural language texts. The non-healthcare applications of NLP include search engines, tagging, sentiment analysis, and filtering recommendations.

In healthcare, anecdotal evidence suggests (somewhat optimistically) that nearly half of the gathered data is in an unstructured format. That free text may be machine-readable, but not machine-understandable. As NLP improves our ability to figure out the linguistic variations, context, and time references of such information, we will have an incredibly powerful tool for harvesting knowledge.

For now, the main use of NLP in healthcare is in billing (big surprise!), in a field called "Computer Assisted Coding" (CAC). CAC analyzes specific phrases and terms within healthcare documents to produce the most appropriate billing codes for a given case. 3M Health Information Systems, Cerner, OptumInsight, Inc., McKesson, Nuance, and Dolbey Systems are some of the prominent CAC vendors.

Clinical use of NLP is mostly limited to research settings at present, but that's likely to change in the next few years. Applications based on NLP have real potential to upend clinical workflows. For instance, NLP can analyze clinical notes to identify patients with intractable epilepsy, and help flag them as potential candidates for neurosurgery. Or detect adverse effects of drugs from the text of discharge summaries, diagnose depression, monitor the rise of hospital-acquired infections... the clinical use cases of NLP-based pattern matching are endless.

Besides giants like Nuance.com, several companies are vying for a share of the healthcare NLP space. For e.g.: Clinithink.com, SyTrue.com, QPIDHealth.com and HealthFidelity.com (based on Columbia University's "Medical Language Extracting and Encoding," or MedLEE, engine).

6

Epilogue

6.1. Tea Leaves

Previous sections covered some key technology-related trends *within* the healthcare industry. At the same time, there are several mega-trends happening *outside* the industry that will end up affecting the healthcare field. This section looks at some of the fundamental technologies likely to reshape healthcare going forward.

Assessing the applications of an emerging technology can induce flights of imagination, but remains a largely speculative undertaking. Even so, it's thrilling to interpret the patterns in the tea leaves swirling around the healthcare industry's cup.

Cloud, Mobile

They may be old news in the larger tech industry but healthcare is still catching up to these two trends. Most established enterprise solutions still exist in a client-server architecture, although the biggest vendors have made consistent strides in the last few years toward a more Software-as-a-Service model. Fortunately, health startups have nearly always gone this route by default.

Similarly, mobile has been an afterthought for enterprise vendors, and major EHR players have a long way to go. The BYOD (bring-your-own-device) trend has also failed to get much traction in clinical organizations. Nevertheless, there is a lot of lip service given to both trends in executive and marketing circles. Real adoption is only going to improve in the future.

Wearable Tech, IoT

The general pattern for this category is pretty clear now: Reliable *sensors* close to the body gather some physiological data, that data is interpreted in the *cloud* based on some logic, and the derived *insights* are used to sell personal and social analytics or professional services.

Variations of this "sensors-cloud-insights" framework are used in nearly all wearable gadgets in the market today. Thanks to marketing successes like Fitbit and Apple Watch, mainstream consumers are now aware that a device worn on the body (wrist, primarily) can actually serve as a constant connection to a health context (activity or sleep, primarily). That widespread market education was perhaps the biggest cleared obstacle for pending innovative ideas that could change the game for niche health conditions. Potential medical uses of wearables include monitoring epileptic seizures, enabling self-driven physical therapy exercises after joint surgery, assisting in recovery from stroke paralysis, or monitoring progression of Parkinson's disease tremors.

Wearables will also play an important role in telemedicine applications, as we discussed in section 5.2. Micro-Electro-Mechanical Systems (MEMS) sensors are cheap and reliable ways to monitor metrics like activity, sleep, heart rate, breathing, and oxygen saturation. Today their market applications are chasing generic, somewhat unoriginal value propositions like sports performance, stress reduction, and wellness. But there is no doubt that this spectrum of consumer-recordable physiological metrics is only going to increase. Their applications will become more targeted and utilitarian, rather than just superficial benchmarking.

It's better to lump the Internet of Things (IoT) trend along with Wearables because its end result is the same for health. They both produce a highly detailed, continuous view of what is going on with an individual and his/her surroundings. A smart refrigerator can perhaps give a count of snack-runs, or even display a healthy recipe based on what food is inside. A smart thermostat can be taught to regulate night temperature for the best sleep. The former can help with a diabetic's lifestyle and the latter can decrease the chance of migraines. The list of such potential use cases is almost endless, but each is very plausible.

As patients generate continuous on-the-go insights about their health and environment, it will create new evidence datasets for care providers. This wealth of information can change some of the guidelines by which medicine is conventionally practiced.

Virtual Reality, Augmented Reality

It's no longer the stuff of science fiction. High-profile projects like Microsoft's HoloLens, Facebook's Oculus Rift, Google's Glass, and MagicLeap.com have all contributed to the feasibility of immersive simulation (VR) and digital overlays on the physical world (AR). Some of these devices are projected to hit the market in 2016. After the expected hiccups are overcome, this new interaction mode will change the norms around information visualization and communication.

All that is bound to impact healthcare, too. Researchers have already experimented with using VR for better pain management and AR to simulate a training environment for complicated operations. The scope of VR/AR is immense and has the potential to force a rethinking of most clinical interactions. A stellar example is using VR headsets to distract children who need a central venous line placed in their body (a tricky, invasive procedure that can go south if the child doesn't stay still and calm).

3D Printing

It was hyped nearly a decade ago in the common press and failed to deliver transformation as quickly or widely as everyone hoped. But the last 2–3 years have seen 3D printing become cheaper and more reliable, as the field seems to enter the "Slope of Enlightenment" phase of Gartner's Hype Cycle. As 3D printing moves beyond just the hobbyists, commercial healthcare is experiencing some mind-boggling applications.

The first 3D-printed prosthetic jaw was implanted in 2012 in the Netherlands. In 2014, physicians at Brigham and Women's Hospital in Boston used 3D-printed models of a patient's head for planning a face transplantation surgery. That same year Dutch surgeons at the University Medical Center Utrecht replaced the skull of a 22-year-old woman with a 3D-printed plastic dome, and Peking University physicians printed and implanted the first 3D vertebra into the spine of a bone cancer patient.

Today, several companies are creating 3D-printed custom casts and prosthetics. The non-profit EnablingTheFuture.org has created an amazing community of individual 3D printer owners who create free 3D-printed hands and arms for those in need of an upper limb assistive device.

As the range of materials expands, costs drop, and printing becomes faster, we'll see more and more applications in health. 3D-printing medical models and custom surgical guides will be a standard step in the process for complicated operations like jaw reconstructions and cranial implants. It will replace the current slow method of creating prosthetics with molds and hand-painted materials. Researchers are already printing actual human cells from a 3D printer, so making transplantable organs from scratch may very well be our incredible future.

Nanotech

The last two decades have yielded a number of consumer product innovations based on nanotechnology. Sharper TV displays, scratch-resistant car bumpers, better sports equipment, stain-resistant clothes, and fast charging batteries are all miracles of matter manipulation at an incredibly small scale.

Healthcare is the next frontier. Since 2001, California-based Proteus.com has been working on ingestible nanosensors that detect if the pill has reached the patient's stomach. Google's Life Sciences group (now called Verily.com) announced in 2014 that it was working on disease-detecting nanoparticles. In late 2015, the FDA accepted an application for the first drug and device combination: Otsuka Pharmaceutical's ABILIFY® (for mental illness) comes embedded with the Proteus sensor. Elsewhere, researchers have already demonstrated human organs-on-chip that can serve as accurate human organ models for drug development. These "Biomimetic Microsystems" make it easier to test efficacies, detect toxicities and model disease progression.

Nanoparticles can be tuned to pass biological barriers, target specific tissue, or appear in a certain visual way during imaging. Nanomedicine is increasingly emerging from research and make personalized treatment a reality.

Drones, Autonomous Vehicles

Unmanned aerial vehicle (drone) technology has been applied to weather detection, 3D mapping landscapes, monitoring wildlife, farming, warfare, and law enforcement. There are more and more press stories about using drones for commercial package deliveries, humanitarian relief, and rescue operations. Drones capable of following their owners autonomously are already in the hands of hobbyists. The past couple of years have seen investments rise, costs plummet, regulations clarify, and social norms emerge. The era of airborne robots with sensors has begun.

This rapid evolution has started to stretch the physical boundaries of the health industry as well. In 2014, a prototype drone for emergency assistance was created for quickly delivering defibrillators to where they were needed. In 2015, DHL announced that it would use a drone to deliver medication to an isolated German island in the North Sea.

Drones that track and follow a patient autonomously can assist in monitoring and safety. They can provide a cheap and reliable means of transporting medical supplies in geographically challenging locations. This technology can truly revolutionize the public health and emergency medicine industries.

Autonomous vehicles may induce similarly massive societal shifts that change the way we live and operate as a community. Aside from changing auto insurance and ownership norms, the availability of driverless transport may change how health services are delivered. Today a smartphone application can only tackle the virtual aspects (like scheduling, billing, and reviews) of on-demand medical concierge services. But driverless cars and dedicated lanes can change how an urgent pediatrician visit, regular physical therapy appointment or emergency medical technician service is delivered. A great deal needs to come together to make these changes a reality (including regulations) but none of it seems infeasible or overly futuristic.

More miracles

Before the above-mentioned trends can find solid footing, more are appearing on the horizon. Each has the same odd composition: buoyed by hype and speculation, yet grounded firmly in powerful technology development that is fundamentally solid and imminent.

For example, take the extraordinary technology called "Blockchain" that underpins the infamous virtual currency Bitcoin. Blockchain is a machine-based way of creating irrefutable trust between participants, without the need for a central authority. The fundamental innovation here is a shared and trusted public ledger that no single user controls but all can inspect. Today, Blockchain is disrupting the hyper-regulated world of finance. That kind of tamper-proof record keeping can also change how PHRs, HIEs, billing, consent, and auditing work in healthcare.

Another example is the indomitable progress of machine learning. It's easier for Google to find cat videos or recognize faces because of such technology. Using that technology to extract knowledge from unlabeled data without prior training has huge implications for healthcare. Detecting minute abnormalities in radiology images, finding a pattern that suggests an obscure disease in long-term data, and predicting an imminent outbreak of a communicable disease are all examples of complex pattern recognition in a highly variable and large dataset.

6.2. Vision or Delusion?

Given that these trends are constantly evolving, it is foolhardy to extrapolate any permanent conclusions. The collective emergence of these paradigm-shifting technologies is what makes the present moment special, however. What comes next is going to be transformative at best and temporarily distracting at worst. Either way, we'll need to deal with a lot of change in healthcare.

The Greek philosopher Socrates was vehemently against the-then new trend of written text. Real knowledge, Socrates said, can only be gathered via dialogue; through a give-and-take of questions and answers where ideas are interrogated until knowledge is truly understood. His disciple Plato agreed that books were a bad idea. Thousands of years later, with the benefit of hindsight, we can now laugh at this anxiety over the impact of written text. Today's amazing assembly of new technologies is perhaps another Socratic moment in societal evolution.

If even celebrated scholars fell short, it's clear that most of us have limited capacity to judge the permanency of mega-trends. The fundamental truth is that technology-induced paradigm shifts are inevitable. Business models and sociocultural norms will always rearrange around a new status quo and make old assumptions invalid.

Today, many innovators are looking for problems they can solve in health. It's our individual choice to view their adoption and experimentation efforts as either visionary or delusional. In the words of the famous magician Joseph Dunninger, "For those who believe, no explanation is necessary; for those who do not believe, no explanation will suffice.

6.3. Entrepreneurship

6.3.1. The Startup Ecosystem

Startups are hard and entrepreneurs don't get the luxury of long runways. Networking (a.k.a. hustling) is the dark art that is required for any startup, and is even more important in healthcare. The list below notes a few stereotype personalities that an upcoming health entrepreneur may encounter. At the risk of being judgmental, it provides some mental rules-of-thumb to keep entrepreneurship interactions more productive.

Fake Mentors

There are plenty of self-proclaimed mentors fishing around to be an advisor to a nascent startup. They end up consuming precious equity and not doing much except making unfruitful introductions. Amassing a huge collection of startups to "advise," fake mentors hope for at least one of their advisees making a notable exit.

Typically, fake mentors in healthcare are physicians looking to diversify beyond the usual clinical persona. Otherwise they tend to be senior executives from big corporations or researchers from academia. Lawyers tend to oblige too, because a lot of their value-add is in doing boilerplate legal work like company incorporation or patent filing (most offer to defer their professional fees until a funding milestone occurs). Even though an offer of guidance may feel flattering, try to pick mentors as carefully as your employees.

Aimless Networking Junkies

They are not entrepreneurs, but enjoy pretending to be one. You will find them floating around at most networking events. The boisterous ones stand out by consistently asking sensationalistic questions during the Q&A sessions of an event. For example, in 2014, that meant bringing up the topic of Google Glass, or worse, wearing one while mentioning it. Sometimes they start local meetup groups that attract other junkies as an audience. Either way, stay away from them if you can, as they are largely a waste of an entrepreneur's time.

Incubator Gators

This appears to be the fastest growing category, especially in relation to health. Existing tech incubators/accelerators like YCombinator.com and Techstars.com have started indulging in health-focused startups. A pack of health-tech-specific incubators have surfaced recently, led by RockHealth.com, HealthboxAccelerator.com, BluePrintHealth.org, and StartupHealth.com. Traditional hospitals systems, pharma companies, insurers, and state-funded organizations have also jumped in solo or with industry partnerships to force their entry into the innovation realm in this way. For example, New York's DigitalHealthAccelerator.com and Stanford's StartX.com/med. A CHCF report found more than 90 dedicated health incubators in late 2014.[40]

It's advisable to approach only those incubators that have good portfolio companies and take fair equity (should be single-digit in most cases). Think twice before signing up with a program that invests cash and then takes some of it back as tuition or rent. Realize that going with a purebred tech incubator means that you won't get the clinical network that comes with a health-focused one. On the other hand, most incubators started by health organizations will have minimal knowledge about creating engaging digital experiences or scaling solutions to millions of end users.

The idealist entrepreneur might argue that great ideas thrive anywhere, but my personal recommendation for health startups would be to favor San Francisco, New York, and Boston as locations (in that order). Talented team members and influential investors tend to be clustered together in these locations, making it easier for the entrepreneur to execute. Add San Diego to the end of the list if your product has a significant medical device context.

Event Managers

Trends come and go, but people in this category are the ones that always finish laughing all the way to the bank. These are ex-networking junkies who have developed an ability to spot the next industry buzzword that can be turned into a conference. Perhaps this is why new technology topics are often long on events and short on substance.

As an healthcare entrepreneur, you should strive to know the Event Manager types. More importantly, let them know your specialty and startup focus. One day you will need to land a speaker opportunity that builds your startup's brand at one of these events.

Evangelists

These are the people who genuinely care about a topic, be it a technology or some aspect of entrepreneurship. Usually they are ex-entrepreneurs holding weird titles like "Developer Evangelist," and displaying no direct affiliation with healthcare. They never explicitly market themselves but still build popularity through great blog posts and thoughtful speeches. Their LinkedIn profile or online resume often feels unkempt and haphazard, as if they don't want to be taken too seriously.

Evangelists are nothing but good news for entrepreneurs. A word of caution though, about a peculiar sub-category of *One-Hit-Wonder Evangelists*. These are ex-entrepreneurs with one or more good exits in the past that have forever eliminated their need to hold a paid job. They always evangelize something (anything) in order to keep feeling relevant in the domain. They can do damage to startups because of their constrained thinking.

Other conventions and personalities

The stereotyped bigotry of authoritative clinical experts (a.k.a. "The God Complex") is often dramatized in stories and anecdotes. Unfortunately, with the rise of technology as a disruptive force, that same stereotype is often reflected in the personality of tech legends who tend to dismiss anything and anyone that is already entrenched in healthcare. For example, famous venture capitalist Vinod Khosla often concludes in his speeches that true disruption can only come from those who are outsiders to an industry. He is entitled to his opinion, but making generalized rules for innovation seems like an inherently contradictory act. Technology entrepreneurship has laid out baselines for disruptive entrepreneurship but perhaps health will teach us how to gracefully evolve the art further. Beware of hyperbolic legends who can distort reality and send you chasing mirages.

6.3.2. Business Models

New ideas surface every day, but not all have a clear way to generate revenue. Viable business models may not be a necessity to launch an idea in the internet age but long-term survival depends on having one.

Below is a list of the different ways healthcare startups have attempted to generate revenue. Note that the categorizations of noted examples are not absolute because a company may qualify for more than one. Also, business models are not publicized, so there are assumptions made in some cases.

- *Broker*: The idea is to bring buyers and sellers together, create a marketplace, and charge a fee to facilitate transactions. Example: AmericanWell.com, Vitals.com, ZocDoc.com, GetInsured.com, Care.com.

- *Subscription*: Charging periodic fees for access to a service or product. Consumer-grade coaching services frequently use this model. Examples: Wello.com, GoLantern.com, Arivale.com, MyHealthDIRECT.com, Amion.com.

- *Pay-as-you-go*: Unlike subscriptions (which are a flat periodic fee), this model charges consumers based on actual usage. This used to be the least popular choice but has seen a revival in the API and telemedicine era. Examples: Eligible.com, DoctorOnDemand.com.

- *License*: Charging a flat fee based on criteria other than just time interval, like the number of active concurrent users. Examples: ArchimedesModel.com, Within3.com, WellDoc.com, Apixio.com, Jiff.com, HealthLoop.com, DrFirst.com, Welltok.com.

- *Advertising*: This is a popular and familiar choice. The company creates free content and derives revenue from advertisers who want access to the viewer's attention. Examples: DailyStrength.com, PsychCentral.com, Healthline.com, PracticeFusion.com, MedHelp.com, Phreesia.com.

- *Information Reseller*: These companies foster a user community with the aim of collecting data about them in aggregate. They sell such population-level data to third parties who mine and discover trends relevant to their offerings. Almost all online social networks related to health would belong in this category. Examples: Sermo.com, PatientsLikeMe.com, Medscape.com, Doximity.com.

- *One-time Sale*: Companies that sell a product or service for a one-time charge. Most wearables and direct-to-consumer testing services will fit in this category. Examples: Fitbit.com, Misfit.com, Withings.com, Navigenics.com, 23andMe.com.

Besides the above list, new companies may choose to be a *Not-for-profit*, i.e. focused on greater good and generally supported by grants or voluntary contributions. Example: Healthmap.org, BensFriends.org, Watsi.org. Others choose to remain free while they figure things out. Like FreeMD.com.

6.3.3. Working with Enterprises

Approaching them

If you are starting a company in healthcare, it's naïve to assume that you'll never need to work with an incumbent enterprise Health IT system like an EHR or an HIE. Even if your startup is a direct-to-consumer offering, all roads eventually lead to the doorstep of established organizations (like hospitals or clinics) which are run on enterprise-grade technology. And for the next 10 years, working with those vendors is not going to be as easy as finding APIs or interface documentation and smoothly aligning with them. That level of externalization and sharing incentive just doesn't exist today. Sadly, enterprise systems are (and will be) the place where health information goes to die.

The clichéd conclusion about these systems (specially EHRs) is that they are evil data hoarders, refusing to share patient information with other systems. But look closely and you'll find that image to be a reflection of their customer's default behaviors. So if you'd like to approach a big Health IT vendor for integration, do it through their customers. The one thing all big enterprise vendors cherish is their marquee customer accounts. If enough customers push, mountains like Epic and Cerner can move.

Convincing your customer to push for integrating your solution with their enterprise software is the real challenge. And although that decision must first be vetted by the clinical leadership, the real gatekeepers often reside in the IT organization.

IT departments in healthcare face the daunting task of answering to multiple stakeholders with conflicting priorities. Often they are in the same room with different clinical champions, each passionate about their own cause, demanding IT support and action. The IT department's usual work is a continuous stream of installations and upgrades punctuated by fire drills of system issues and user complaints. Imagine how they feel about adding another vendor to their attention stream and employee bandwidth. Especially if that new vendor is smaller and relatively unknown, as compared to their usual partner.

Getting a high rank on the priority list of your customer's IT department is what moves the needle. Use clinical thought leaders to validate your idea and lobby your integration needs, then offer to do all of the heavy lifting and make things easy for the IT team.

Pilot Paralysis

One major caveat in using health organizations as initial customers is what I call the "Pilot Paralysis." The last few years have seen scores of young technology companies kicking off ambitious projects with big-name health organizations and never recovering from it. These pilots suffer problems like vague requirements, political wrangling, design intrusion, highly specific content, and painfully slow decision-making. What ends up being created is a bespoke solution for one customer and not something that can be generalized for the market. The startup usually doesn't get paid anything and can end up sharing intellectual property and/or equity with the organization.

For startups, partnering with a high-profile health organization can be like a kitten getting hugged by a bear. It feels safe and warm at first, but can quickly become suffocating. If your startup is doing a pilot with an established organization, always keep showcasing to that partner's peers and ask them one simple question: "Will you pay for this?" If you don't get a positive answer, think about gracefully bowing out of the pilot.

For better or worse, healthcare is not an industry where radical changes happen quickly or widely. There are simply too many social, political, and emotional vectors that need to move together for sustainable, widespread change to happen rapidly. While we can wait for technology adoption miracles to happen, it's more practical for entrepreneurs to take a subtle, nuanced approach that gently realigns and guides the system rather than disrupts it. Iterate often and plan for small, short pilots with multiple organizations for each release.

6.3.4. It's Time.

"The necessary and sufficient condition for the downfall of an ideological society is a free exchange of ideas within it." This quote embodies the potential impact startups can have in health.

Medical practitioners can be thought of as a society with common thinking and mannerisms. With years of rigorous training, clinicians are expected to possess knowledge about disease causation and treatment. This highly valuable information is what enables them to provide expert care and get paid in return. A patient, on the other hand, doesn't know as much about the science and art of health.

This type of information inequity exists in a number of professions. Consider lawyers or car mechanics, for example. These too are professions where money changes hands because the consumer is not as well informed as the expert providing the service.

And therein lies the transformative power of information. What if anyone could read a simple guide on how to file a utility patent or change a spark plug? Then consumers could self-service some fraction of their needs. By reducing information inequity, what was expert service yesterday becomes a commodity do-it-yourself task today.

To be fair, mere information access doesn't make one an expert. Watching appendectomy videos doesn't qualify the viewer to be a surgeon. Skills and training play a vital role too. Through experience, experts master the ability to execute tasks with predictable results. But information remains an important part of the foundation throughout, constantly leveling the playing field between experts and beginners.

In any domain, a gradual commoditization of the simpler peripheral workflows and knowledge is inevitable. It happens even faster in domains where both demand and technology are evolving at a rapid pace. Small wonder then that there are DIY services ranging from filing taxes online to kits for converting your car into a hybrid electric vehicle. Unfortunately, healthcare's evolution seems to be sub-optimal in this context. Progress has been made, but perhaps not in the areas of greatest concern. Today it's easy to self-manage teeth whitening but still nearly impossible to price-shop for an X-ray or find verified physician reviews.

All that will change within the next decade.

For far too long, the knowledge of care had been held captive on paper or in expert minds. Now that health information is going digital, it can be shared easily and widely. That free exchange of health information disrupts the orthodox and ideological nature of the industry. The resulting innovation will transform the captive, paternalistic way of medicine that has weighed down progress for many decades. There has never been a better time to be an entrepreneur in healthcare.

Acknowledgments

Writing a book, as I've discovered first-hand, is the most intense way to experience self-doubt and the highly subjective analysis of others. Surviving authorhood is completely dependent on having a great support network. I'd like to thank some of the exceptional people who helped make this book possible. Without their constant encouragement and assistance, I would have never gone beyond my occasional verbal catharsis about the state of Health IT.

I'm especially grateful to Adam Schlifke, MD, MBA, who put in an inordinate amount of time going through the content. His suggestions were invaluable in shaping this book. I'd also like to thank the following for their suggestions:

- Naveen Rao (Managing Director, Patchwise Labs and Editor, Tincture)
- Members of the Shah Lab team at the Center for Biomedical Informatics Research at Stanford (shahlab.stanford.edu)

I'm indebted to my mother for supporting my unconventional career decisions. She had the foresight to gauge the importance of computers in healthcare delivery nearly 17 years ago and gave me the confidence to start exploring the then-unknown space of Health IT.

Finally, this book could not exist without the unyielding support of my wife. Her belief in my capabilities is what keeps me working on seemingly impossible ideas and visions. Without her, life would be extremely ordinary and predictable.

About the Author

After finishing medical school in 2001, Pallav veered into a technology-focused career that enabled him to work at medical device companies, health insurers, hospital systems, and startups.

His non-clinical career started with *GE Healthcare*, with roles in services, engineering, R&D, and marketing organizations of the Electronic Health Record (EHR) business. During that time, he also served as an Instructor for the graduate Medical Informatics program at *Northwestern University* in Illinois. Subsequently, he joined *Kaiser Permanente* to work on Clinical Data Analytics and Population Health Management technology initiatives. He then transitioned to *UnitedHealth Group* and led the Product Management team for Health Information Exchange (HIE) solutions. Before leaving the corporate world in 2014, he was the Director of Health IT Interoperability initiatives at *Omnicell, Inc.*

Pallav received his MBA from Northwestern University, a Masters in Medical Informatics from Columbia University, and a Bachelors of Medicine and Surgery (MBBS) from Delhi University, India. He currently lives in Menlo Park, California and continues to indulge in the Health IT entrepreneurship space. Find out more about him on:

- LinkedIn: www.linkedin.com/in/pallav
- Facebook: www.facebook.com/pallavsharda
- Twitter: www.twitter.com/pallavsharda
- Quora: www.quora.com/pallav-sharda
- Personal Websites: pallav.shardas.com, multiplyd.com

References

1. Bloomberg. *Health Care's $605 Billion Buying Binge May Slow in 2016.* Accessed April 25, 2016.http://bloom.bg/1OM1g5S.

2. Institute of Medicine. *The Computer-based Patient Record.* http://www.nap.edu/read/5306.

3. Institute of Medicine. *To Err Is Human.* http://www.nap.edu/read/9728.

4. Blumenthal and Tavenner. *The Meaningful Use Regulation for Electronic Health Records.* New England Journal of Medicine 363 (2010):501-504. doi: 10.1056/NEJMp1006114.

5. ONC. Data Brief No. 23. *Adoption of Electronic Health Record Systems among U.S. Non-Federal Acute Care Hospitals.* Accessed April 25, 2016.
https://www.healthit.gov/policy-researchers-implementers/briefs

6. CMS. *Hospital EHR Vendors Data (March 2015).* Accessed April 25, 2016.
http://dashboard.healthit.gov/quickstats/pages/FIG-Vendors-of-EHRs-to-Participating-Hospitals.php

7. CMS. *Health Care Professional EHR Vendors Data (March 2015).* Accessed April 25, 2016.
http://dashboard.healthit.gov/quickstats/pages/FIG-Vendors-of-EHRs-to-Participating-Professionals.php

8. It's not a perfect analogy, of course. ACH Network is a batch-processing, store-and-forward system that doesn't retain a copy for itself. HIEs tend to store a snapshot of patient's information that is of common interest to all participants.

9. Starr. *Smart technology, stunted policy: developing health information networks*. Health Affairs Vol.16 No.3 (May 1997): 91-105. doi:10.1377/hlthaff.16.3.91.

10. AHRQ. *Trends in Health Information Exchanges*. Accessed April 25, 2016.
https://innovations.ahrq.gov/perspectives/trends-health-information-exchanges.

11. Blumenthal. *Launching HITECH*. New England Journal of Medicine 362 (2010):382-385.
doi:10.1056/NEJMp0912825.

12. ONC. *2011 Edition Test Methods*. Accessed April 25, 2016.
http://www.healthit.gov/policy-researchers-implementers/2011-edition-approved-test-methods.

13. ONC. *2014 Edition Test Methods*. Accessed April 25, 2016.
http://www.healthit.gov/policy-researchers-implementers/2014-edition-final-test-method.

14. ONC. *About the ONC Health IT Certification Program*. Accessed April 25, 2016.
http://www.healthit.gov/policy-researchers-implementers/about-onc-hit-certification-program.

15. ONC. *How to attain Meaningful Use*. Accessed April 25, 2016.
http://www.healthit.gov/providers-professionals/how-attain-meaningful-use.

16. Leavitt Partners. *Projected Growth of Accountable Care Organizations*. Accessed April 25, 2016.
http://leavittpartners.com/2015/12/projected-growth-of-accountable-care-organizations.

17. Healthcare IT News, September 2012. *EHR vendors among Forbes' richest.* Accessed April 25, 2016.
http://www.healthcareitnews.com/news/ehr-vendors-among-forbes-richest.

18. Kaiser Family Foundation. *2015 Employer Health Benefits Survey.* Accessed April 25, 2016.
http://kff.org/report-section/ehbs-2015-summary-of-findings.

19. American Medical News. *One answer to EMR data entry: Hire a scribe to do it.* Accessed April 25, 2016.
http://www.amednews.com/article/20080714/business/307149998/5/

20. Office of Inspector General, HHS. *Not all recommended fraud safeguards have been implemented in hospital EHR technology.* Accessed April 25, 2016.
http://oig.hhs.gov/oei/reports/oei-01-11-00570.pdf.

21. Pederson et al. *ASHP national survey of pharmacy practice in hospital setting: Prescribing and transcribing-2013.* American Journal of Health-System Pharmacy, Vol.71, No.11(2014): 924-942.doi: 10.2146/ajhp140032.

22. Institute of Medicine. *Preventing Medication Errors.* Accessed April 25, 2016.
http://www.nap.edu/read/11623.

23. ONC Data Brief No. 18, July 2014. *E-Prescribing Trends in the United States.* Accessed April 25, 2016.
http://healthit.gov/sites/default/files/oncdatabriefe-prescribingincreases2014.pdf.

24. CMS. *Emergency Medical Treatment & Labor Act (EMTALA)*. Accessed April 25, 2016. https://www.cms.gov/Regulations-and-Guidance/Legislation/EMTALA.

25. Schuur and Venkatesh. *The Growing Role of Emergency Departments in Hospital Admissions*. New England Journal of Medicine 367 (2012):391-393. doi:10.1056/NEJMp1204431.

26. Wilson and Cutler. *Emergency Department Profits Are Likely To Continue As The Affordable Care Act Expands Coverage*. Health Affairs Vol. 33, No. 5 (2014):792-799. doi:10.1377/hlthaff.2013.0754.

27. Andrews. *Emergency Care, But Not At A Hospital*. Kaiser Health News. Accessed April 25, 2016. http://khn.org/news/michelle-andrews-on-hospital-er-alternatives/

28. Stol et al. *Technology diffusion of anesthesia information management systems into academic anesthesia departments in the United States*. Anesthesia & Analgesia Journal 118 (2014 March):644-50. doi: 10.1213/ANE.0000000000000055.

29. ONC. *What is HIE?*. Accessed April 25, 2016. http://www.healthit.gov/providers-professionals/health-information-exchange/what-hie.

30. ONC. *State HIE Program Measures Dashboard*. Accessed April 25, 2016. http://www.healthit.gov/policy-researchers-implementers/state-hie-program-measures-dashboard.

31. ONC Nationwide Health Information Network (NwHIN). Accessed April 25, 2016.

http://www.healthit.gov/policy-researchers-implementers/nationwide-health-information-network-nwhin.

32. CDC. Immunization Information Systems (IIS). Accessed April 25, 2016.
http://www.cdc.gov/vaccines/programs/iis/contacts-registry-staff.html.

33. Workgroup for Electronic Data Interchange. *Transactions & Electronic Data Interchange.* Accessed April 25, 2016.
http://www.wedi.org/topics/transactions-electronic-data-interchange.

34. ASTM International. *Standard Specification for Continuity of Care Record (CCR).* Accessed on April 25, 2016.
http://www.astm.org/Standards/E2369.htm.

35. Guttmacher Institute. An Overview of Minors' Consent Law. Accessed April 25, 2016.
http://www.guttmacher.org/statecenter/spibs/spib_OMCL.pdf.

36. Gartner. *Interpreting Technology Hype.* Accessed April 25, 2016.
http://www.gartner.com/technology/research/methodologies/hype-cycle.jsp

37. Federation of State Medical Boards. Report accessed on April 25, 2016.
https://www.fsmb.org/Media/Default/PDF/FSMB/Advocacy/FSMB_Telemedicine_Policy.pdf.

38. National Conference of State Legislatures. White paper accessed on April 25, 2016.
http://www.ncsl.org/documents/health/telehealth2015.pdf.

39. FDA MedWatch. *Viracept: Important information for prescribers.* Accessed April 25, 2016. http://www.fda.gov/downloads/Safety/MedWatch/SafetyInfor mation/SafetyAlertsforHumanMedicalProducts/UCM154880.pdf

40. CHCF. *Survival of the Fittest: Health Care Accelerators Evolve Toward Specialization.* Accessed April 25, 2016. http://www.chcf.org/publications/2014/10/survival-fittest-accelerators.

www.beforedisrupting.com

33017611R00131

Made in the USA
Middletown, DE
26 June 2016